# The Music Teacher's Companion

## A Practical Guide

Paul Harris and Richard Crozier

The Associated Board of the Royal Schools of Music

First published in 2000 by
The Associated Board of the Royal Schools of Music (Publishing) Limited
24 Portland Place, London W1B 1LU, United Kingdom

© 2000 by The Associated Board of the Royal Schools of Music

International Edition ISBN 1 86096 191 6
Malaysia Edition ISBN 1 86096 220 3
Singapore Edition ISBN 1 86096 221 1
UK Edition ISBN 1 86096 219 X

AB 2763

All rights reserved. No part of this publication may be reproduced,
stored in a retrieval system, or transmitted in any form or by any means,
electronic, mechanical, photocopying, recording, or otherwise, without
the prior permission of the copyright owner. This specifically does not
apply to the forms on page 133 onwards, which may be photocopied
without prior permission.

A CIP catalogue for this book is available from The British Library.

Chapters 7 and 8 draw on materials contained within Paul Harris's
publications *Improve your sight-reading!* and *Improve your scales!* published by
Faber Music Ltd.

Illustrations © Martin Shovel
Design and setting by Hilite Design & Reprographics Limited, Southampton
Printed in England by Caligraving Limited, Thetford, Norfolk

# Contents

Introduction     vii

## Section One   The Essence of Teaching

**Chapter 1   Teachers and Pupils**     3
  Effective teaching     3
  Making assumptions     3
  The teacher     4
  The pupil     6
  Assessing potential pupils     7
  Pupil Profile Forms     8

**Chapter 2   Age and Approach**     9
  Musical experiences for the very young     9
  The growing child     11
  Early burn-out     11
  The developing child     12
  Adolescence     13
  Teaching adults     15

**Chapter 3   Lessons**     17
  Evolving a curriculum     17
  Teaching style     18
  Learning styles     19
  Basic principles of teaching     19
  Lesson presentation     21
    Expectation     21
    Guidance     22
  Lesson content     22
  The first lessons     23
  Lesson etiquette     25

**Chapter 4   Motivation**     27
  Defining motivation     27
  Motivation in practice     28
  Poor motivation     30
  Transferring responsibility as a form of motivation     31

**Chapter 5   Monitoring Your Work**     33
  Language – praise and criticism     33
  Language – technical terms     34
  Planning and preparation     34
  Music and general content     34
  Time for reflection…     35
    On a specific pupil     35
    On a specific lesson     35

**Chapter 6   Teaching Rhythm**     37
  What is rhythm?     37
  Have I got rhythm?     38
  Teaching pulse     39
  The vital importance of subdivision     40
  Teaching rhythmic patterns     42
    Word rhythms     43
  Teaching counting     43
    When is 'one' not 'one'?     43
  Pulse and tempo     44

### Chapter 7  Teaching Sight-Reading — 45
Why learn to sight-read? — 45
The reading process — 45
The basic elements of sight-reading — 46
  Pitch — 46
  Rhythm — 46
  Combining pitch with rhythm — 47
Sight-reading as a multi-task activity — 47
  Remembering the key signature — 48
  Looking ahead — 48
  Observing dynamic markings and other marks of expression and articulation — 49
  Fingering — 49
  Developing an aural understanding of the music — 49
  Having some understanding of the harmony — 50
How to teach sight-reading — 50
  Making mental plans — 51
  Skim-reading — 52
Sight-reading in examinations — 52

### Chapter 8  Teaching Scales — 53
Scales and technique — 53
Teaching strategies — 54
  By ear or not by ear — 54
  Scale learning without scales! — 55
  Making friends with scales — 57
  The perfect scale — 57
Practice strategies — 58
Teaching modes — 58

### Chapter 9  Teaching Aural Skills — 59
The point of aural training — 59
The musical ear — 59
An ever-present ingredient — 60
Using the voice — 61
Playing and singing in tune — 62
Memory — 62
Aural and memory — 63
Specific aural tests — 63
  Clapping or tapping back a rhythmic phrase — 63
  Singing back a melody — 64
  Identifying intervals, cadences, chords, major/minor etc. — 64
  Perceptive listening — 64
  Spotting mistakes — 65

### Chapter 10  Improvising and Composing — 67
What is improvisation? — 67
Why improvise? — 68
Practical uses of improvisation and working with notation — 68
  As part of aural training — 68
  Improvising exercises to improve technique — 68
  Increasing general musical awareness — 69
  Developing confidence — 69
  Exploring the instrument — 69
  Self-expression through improvisation — 69
  The development of skills required in certain exams — 69
The development of a particular musical genre — 70
From improvising to composing — 70

**Chapter 11 Simultaneous Learning** 71
   The problem 71
   The solution 72
   The simultaneous learning lesson 72
   Making connections 76
   Simultaneous learning for the beginner pupil 77
   The sliding scale 77

**Chapter 12 Group Teaching** 79
   Some background as to why we teach instruments individually 79
   The development of group teaching 80
   Preparing for group teaching 80
   Strategies for group teaching 81
   Simultaneous learning in group teaching and the meaning of progress 82
   The occasional group lesson 83
   Practical considerations 84

**Chapter 13 Teaching Pupils with Special Requirements** 85
   Being musically gifted 85
   Identifying the characteristics 86
   The problem and the solution 87
   Teaching the highly gifted 87
   The ageing prodigy 88
   Pupils with special educational needs 89
      Dyslexia 89
      Dyspraxia 89

## Section Two  Beyond the Lesson

**Chapter 14 Practice** 93
   What is practice? 93
   The principles of good practice 93
   What makes people practise? 95
   What is good practising? 96
      The beginner 96
      The developing player 97
      More advanced players 97
   Practice strategies 98
      The practice room 98
      Pupil's demeanour 98
      Practice content 98
      The practice notebook 98
      The teacher's practice diary 98
      Critical listening 98
      Practice by repetition 99
      'Mechanical' practice 99
      Practising pieces 99
      Practising practice 100
   Pupils who do no practice 100
   Practice and anxiety 100
   Does practice make perfect? 101
   A practice checklist 102

**Chapter 15 Preparation and Performance** 103
   Preparing music for performance 103
      Teaching 'style' 103
      Teaching interpretation 104
   The performance 105
   Performance anxiety 106

| | |
|---|---|
| Playing from memory | 107 |
|   Aural memory | 108 |
|   Kinaesthetic memory | 108 |
|   Intellectual memory | 108 |
|   Photographic (visual) memory | 109 |

## Chapter 16  Examinations — 111
| | |
|---|---|
| The role of grade examinations | 111 |
| Misusing examinations and failure | 112 |
| Preparing pupils for grade examinations | 113 |
| Non-musical factors | 113 |
| The result | 114 |
| After the examination | 115 |
| Grade 8 and beyond | 115 |

## Chapter 17  Competitions and Festivals — 117
| | |
|---|---|
| The advantages of competitions and festivals | 117 |
| The disadvantages and how to deal with them | 118 |
| Preparing pupils | 119 |
| High-profile competitions | 119 |
| The competitive world | 120 |

## Chapter 18  Holiday Courses — 121
| | |
|---|---|
| Orchestral courses | 121 |
| Other courses | 122 |
| Do-it-yourself courses | 122 |

## Chapter 19  What Next? — 125
| | |
|---|---|
| Music college or university? | 125 |
| Getting in | 126 |
| Other careers in music | 127 |

## Chapter 20  Some Professional Considerations — 129
| | |
|---|---|
| Working for yourself | 129 |
| Working in schools | 130 |
| Contractual obligations | 130 |
| The school music curriculum | 131 |

| | |
|---|---|
| Further Reading and References | 132 |
| Attendance Register | 133 |
| Pupil Profile Form | 134 |
| Termly Overview Sheet | 135 |
| Lesson Plan/Record Sheet | 136 |

# Introduction

This book is for all instrumental and singing teachers. Well-established and new teachers will find it equally relevant, whether working at home or in schools, full-time or part-time, teaching individuals or groups. It contains information, advice and a wide range of pragmatic solutions to everyday problems, as well as dealing with issues relating to the quality of teaching and learning that takes place, such as the monitoring of motivation, achievement and progress. It discusses many concepts and strategies that may well have remained unquestioned during years of teaching, and includes some ideas that may surprise or challenge. It also contains forms for lesson plans, pupil profiles, termly overviews and attendance registers, and much other useful information.

Our primary intention is to provide a means to invigorate, broaden and stimulate thought about all aspects of teaching and thus help you to offer the best possible service to your pupils.

The authors wish to thank a number of friends, colleagues and students for their reading of the manuscript, for their challenging and provoking comments and for their encouragement and support.

Paul Harris and Richard Crozier

Section One

# The Essence of Teaching

# Teachers and Pupils

## Effective teaching

Are you an effective teacher? What is effective teaching? Are your lessons effective? Consider these important questions for a few minutes before reading on and make a note of your thoughts.

You might think effective teachers are those whose pupils seem to display both quality of performance and enthusiasm. Surprisingly, this may not always be the case; some pupils manage to maintain their enthusiasm even in the face of the most weary and indifferent teaching. Even if you are well-informed about the theory of teaching, make careful lesson plans and select appropriate material, you might present what could be termed a *good* lesson but it might still fail as an *effective* one.

So what, then, is effective teaching, and how can you be sure that your teaching is always effective? Those teachers who take a real interest in the actual learning processes and who carefully monitor the extent to which their pupils have understood what they are trying to teach can feel confident that they are moving significantly towards effective teaching.

Central to the concept of effective teaching, therefore, is the importance of a two-way dialogue; you should be continually aware of whether or not your pupils are switched-on to what you are teaching. Watch them carefully; often a facial expression or negative body language gives away the fact that a pupil doesn't understand, or has lost interest in, what you are trying to teach. Talk to your pupils; ask them to explain back what you have just taught them. Never, under any circumstances, simply *assume* that your pupil has understood, and thus learnt, something.

## Making assumptions

In teaching, just as in everyday life, making assumptions often inhibits smooth and effective communication. As we go through any day we are continually making assumptions; we assume any comment or action we make is being understood or interpreted just as we intended it to be. Similarly, in making a comment or giving an instruction, we assume the recipient has already understood or assimilated perhaps a whole chain of concepts or skills necessary for the safe receipt of this new information. Remember that what you know and take for granted is all relatively new to your pupils. For example, young pupils may not realize that F and F natural are the same note, or that a rhythm is the same whether the note stem points up or down. When introducing something new, try to be conscious of how each pupil understands and relates it to that already learnt. Be aware of (unspoken) confusion – very few pupils will have the confidence to ask pertinent questions at this stage in their learning. For example, on first encountering a note with a down-stem the pupil may perceive this note as being 'upside-down'. Even though they may not express the concern, they may be worrying about whether this note is played in the same way as 'an ordinary note'. This anxiety may well be undermining the learning process. A few words of explanation will soon put your pupil's mind at ease!

As you begin to think along these lines, many areas of possible misunderstanding will emerge. Get into the habit of asking questions to ensure that fresh or unfamiliar ideas have been understood. Ask your pupils to explain a new musical idea or technical skill back to you. Occasionally you might try some 'role reversal' – ask your pupil to teach you something that you have recently taught them. If you play the part of the 'slow learner' you will really see how well your pupil understands!

**Chapter 5**
Monitoring Your Work

It is essential to revisit and reinforce new concepts and skills many times. Effective teaching will have taken place when pupils can successfully apply what they have learnt. For example, when teaching 'tied notes' begin at a simple level with one kind of tie (say, two crotchets/quarter notes either side of a bar line). Once the pupil has clearly understood the function of a tie, try tying notes of different values – you will soon know whether your teaching has been effective.

## The teacher

There are two distinct but interrelated disciplines central to the teaching of instrumental music. On the one hand we must teach our pupils the skills necessary to play their instruments to the best of their ability, and on the other we must help them to develop their sense of artistry and musicianship. Perhaps the most demanding and stimulating challenge faced by the teacher is to draw from the pupil that subtle ability to communicate something of their innermost self through the medium of musical performance. Without developing musical 'personality', performances will remain uninspired and the central message of the music will not be communicated. In order to bring about these results we need to have a closer look at the teacher.

**Chapter 11**
Simultaneous Learning

> Take a few moments and make a list of all the necessary attributes you feel an effective teacher requires. As you think more deeply you may be surprised to find it to be quite long!

Some of the main components are listed below. They are not in 'order of importance'; after reading them through add any you feel have been omitted and then put the whole list in your own order of importance:

**Knowledge and understanding of instrumental skill** Having a deep knowledge of how to play your instrument and its repertoire is, of course, essential. Simply being able to play well, however, is not sufficient; teaching others involves a great deal of analytical thought and understanding.

**A love of music** This needs no explanation, although perhaps it is important to add that you should be open-minded about all types and styles of music.

**Communication skills** Understanding your instrument and having a love of music must be complemented by the ability to communicate. Pupils are individuals; they learn at their own pace and in their own way. It is a great challenge for a teacher, therefore, to develop a flexibility of approach so that the explanation of concepts and skills and the communication of the much more abstract world of artistic expression will be understood by all.

**Musical imagination** Your own musical imagination, independent of that of your pupils, must be constantly nurtured, and may involve going to hear live performances by other players (or at least listening to recordings). Reading, and generally taking an interest in other artistic media, is also important and inspirational to many musicians.

**Sensitivity** To be an effective teacher you must always be sensitive both to subtle reactions and to the occasional unpredictable or unexpected response of a pupil, either of which may require a sudden change of strategy or approach.

**Administrative skills** Working out timetables, filling out festival and exam forms and dealing with payments for lessons are among the many administrative duties the teacher will have to perform. Pupils (and parents) will appreciate an organized teacher!

**Practical knowledge** There is a vast amount of knowledge instrumental teachers are expected to carry with them: an awareness of the various exam boards and their syllabuses, opportunities for holiday courses and local and national orchestras, piano tuners and good local instrumental technicians, music shops, an awareness of the latest publications from publishers and the availability of scholarships represent just some of the information you may be expected to know. Access to a good library, up-to-date music reference books and the Internet will certainly prove invaluable.

**Personality** Enthusiasm, a methodical mind, a sincere concern for your pupils, a good deal of patience and a sense of humour are all essential qualities for the teacher. In addition, it is important that you have a certain measure of self-esteem and confidence in what you are doing; possessing a certain degree of self-respect will help both to achieve warm and supportive relations with others and to promote the development of a similar self-respect in your pupils. An accepting and rewarding approach to each pupil will enhance their view of themselves as people of worth and thus can have quite a marked influence on the effectiveness of their learning. Also, never underestimate a pupil's ability to 'see through' their teacher; they are in a strong position to perceive and evaluate their teacher's feelings towards them and this is clearly a central factor in the development of the pupil–teacher relationship.

**Ability to inspire, enthuse and encourage** Think back over your own learning experiences and whether you have been inspired by any of your teachers. If you have, consider what it was about their teaching or personality that caused you to be inspired. Of course, no one can be expected to be inspirational all the time, but you do need to keep your pupils interested, motivated and excited about playing music.

> Chapter 4 ➤
> Motivation

**Humility** Although it is for the teacher to be the guiding force, it is salutary to remember that we can still learn from each of our pupils. Successful teaching is often the result of two-way respect.

It would be unrealistic to expect every teacher to possess endless reserves of all the above, but a simple awareness of them is a good point of departure. The relative importance attached to each is really for the individual to decide, for every teacher is an individual and your quest must be to endeavour to forge your own unique style and to respond effectively to all types of pupil.

Teachers should occasionally enter into a situation where they are doing the learning! It is very revealing to find out what learning a new and complex skill actually feels like. Choose a pastime such as chess, bridge, Tai Chi, or perhaps learning a new language, and use the experience to reflect on your own pupils' learning experience.

## The pupil

Learning to play a musical instrument, or to sing, has long been considered one of the most fulfilling and profound talents a young person can develop. Yet it is perhaps regrettable to learn that in a study made by the educationalist Leslie Francis in 1987, music and religious study occupied the lowest position in the child's evaluation of the main curriculum areas. Additionally, there is still a certain stigma attached to 'playing a musical instrument'. In some schools pupils who have to leave an academic lesson to 'go to a music lesson' may still need to learn to cope with a little gentle derision. For those who learn their music out of school this does not present the same problem, though there will be times when they may have to practise rather than pursue a social or leisure activity. So, learning an instrument requires a certain strength of character, and as a teacher it is probably as well to bear this in mind.

There are many different types of pupil and each will require a different approach. Find out why they are learning. Some pupils want to learn because they love the sound their instrument makes or because they love music in general; others learn because they have a sibling or friend who plays, or because a parent or grandparent wants them to. This kind of knowledge is invaluable in helping you to develop your approach. Get to know your pupils; ask them about their interests and hobbies, their brothers and sisters (and, for the younger ones, don't forget their pets!). Your pupils will respond to your teaching all the better for showing this kind of concern.

**Chapter 4**

Motivation

In an ideal world we would always be able to choose our pupils; in reality, more often than not (particularly if we are teaching in schools) we have little or no choice. You should feel able and quite justified, when necessary, to redirect unsuitable pupils (perhaps for physical reasons) to other instruments to avoid frustration and a negative experience for all concerned.

## Assessing potential pupils

If you are lucky enough to have a waiting list and are therefore in a position to interview potential pupils, there are numerous useful strategies to follow. Certain questions should be asked, such as whether sufficient finance is available. Instruments and their upkeep, lessons, music, accessories, exam and festival fees and travelling all add up to make learning an instrument an expensive business.

Depending on the instrument, it is important to take build, hand size and physical stamina into account. Does the child demonstrate a sense of determination, tenacity, enthusiasm and a personality tending to the extrovert? Some aural tests will indicate whether the child has a musical ear. The kind of aural tests you give will depend on their age and musical experience. For the young beginner you might discover whether they can sing back a note in tune, differentiate a rising interval from a falling one, maintain a steady pulse and clap back a simple rhythmic pattern. For the student who has already had some instruction, you may wish to give more comprehensive aural tests.

You might like to ask a potential pupil to have a go at some improvisation.

The whole idea may be entirely new to them, but nevertheless their approach may be very revealing. Ask them to improvise (or simply 'make up') a tune using, say, three notes (CDE for example), or perhaps just the black notes on the piano. Or they may like to sing rather than play. You might play a simple arpeggio accompaniment. Be patient and don't hurry them. By their reaction and their attempt (if they make one) you may discover the pupil to be highly creative, shy or extrovert, thoughtful or impulsive. You may be able to ascertain whether they have a good or poor sense of rhythm, whether they have a good ear, and whether they are willing to try new things or have a rather stubborn nature (which may be interpreted either positively or negatively).

Try not to judge them on the quality of their improvisation, but on their approach to the task. Assuming that the pupil doesn't run out of the room screaming (in which case you might want to think very carefully before taking them on), the results, whatever they may be, could tell you a lot about the pupil and the kind of teaching from which they would most benefit.

Finally, find out what the pupil's (or their parents') expectations are and make sure they are aware of yours. For example, it is important for you to discover if a potential new pupil is not keen to practise *before* taking them on!

## Pupil Profile Forms

When you take on a new pupil you will want to know a certain amount about them. Pupil Profile Forms are useful in compiling such information. There is a blank form for you to photocopy at the back of this book. The top box can be filled in at the pupil's first lesson. The other boxes should be completed as you get to know the pupil better and the whole will be useful as reference for report writing and discussion with parents. You may either like to share this form with the pupil or keep it as a confidential record. This decision will probably influence exactly how honest you are in your assessments!

# Age and Approach

Recent research suggests that everyone is born with some embryonic kind of musical intelligence. Readers who are particularly interested in this are strongly recommended to read *Frames of Mind* by Howard Gardner, in which his theories on 'multiple intelligence' are discussed in detail. In essence, he argues that the brain evinces seven different intelligences, ranging from linguistic and mathematical to spatial and musical. The 'musical intelligence' involves the processing of sound as opposed to language and, in Gardner's opinion, is one of the first intelligences to develop. Thus, given the right conditions, 'nature' seems to provide the basic musical ingredients for 'nurture' to cultivate.

**Further Reading and References**

Those young children who are born into musical families are in a considerably advantaged position: the right conditions are already in place. Music is considered a worthwhile occupation and parents will always be encouraging and prepared to invest both time and money in developing their child's musical interests.

This chapter deals with the changes that occur as children get older and how teachers will constantly need to adjust their approach if their teaching is to be effective and appropriate. The actual methods and strategies of teaching are dealt with in the chapters that follow and these, broadly speaking, can be adapted, with a little imagination, for any age group.

## Musical experiences for the very young

Children of three years or younger are unlikely to play musical instruments, but there may be specialist classes in your area where they can enjoy musical activities that will begin to develop their sense of pulse through movement, and where they can sing and dance. They will probably be introduced to some creative work – improvisation with simple instruments, for example. For the child who shows an interest in music, these early classes can be of enormous benefit. In addition, it is important for parents to be aware of the power of their influence over the very young child. For example, a negative reaction to a young child who is perhaps having fun making random sounds on the piano, or simply banging a drum (or some other noise-producing implement), may be very injurious indeed. 'Stop making that awful noise!' may well put the child off music for life. 'That's interesting – what is it supposed to be? A train, or angry sounds or . . .' is, on the other hand, the kind of response that may awaken the imagination of the proto-musician. In addition, parents who sing to, or with, their children are planting important seeds for future musical growth.

A number of children begin learning instruments between the ages of three and six years. Teachers for this age group tend to be specialists and will understand their particular requirements. Children will have limited powers of concentration and will usually only be able to concentrate on one thing at a time. They will enjoy activity, will often be emotionally volatile and will respond well to creative teaching. Successful teachers should make lessons fun and full of varying activities that will stimulate and engage the minds of their pupils. Simple (but never patronizing) language should be used, and clear explanations given of the tasks set. Teachers should be encouraging and patient and not expect too much.

There are a number of specialist music courses available for the very young, each with a particular emphasis. The Kodály system centres on the voice and develops general musicianship through a very carefully devised and progressive programme. Those brought up in the Kodály method can expect to have quite advanced musicianship skills by their early teens. The Suzuki method is principally for string players, although the piano and flute have also been included. The Yamaha system centres on keyboard playing, and develops a wide range of musicianship skills.

The Dalcroze approach focuses on rhythm and movement. Such classes are well worth considering, especially if the child has a strong enthusiasm for music. Parents who share these early musical experiences with their children will discover them to be both fascinating and stimulating, and will find themselves able to help in a practical and supportive way.

## The growing child

It is between the ages of about six and nine when most young people begin their instrumental training. At this age children often have efficient memories, are very eager to learn but will still probably have a short attention span. Never underestimate their capacity for learning and thirst for knowledge. Set them challenging tasks and expect a lot in return – they are normally not afraid of failure and will always want to 'have a go'.

This is the time you can really lay many of the foundations of playing and musicianship. Thorough teaching at this level is an enormous investment for the future. Lessons will have to be carefully planned to include a variety of activities that will develop musicianship, gradually instil understanding of notation, engender a love of the sound of the instrument and stimulate the child's imagination through creative work. Most young learners need constant and creative reinforcement to maintain their interest and establish strong foundations and a sense of progress. Thus the challenge for the teacher is how to present the same material in a variety of imaginative guises. The repertoire and tutor books used should be carefully chosen, and you will probably have to provide additional material yourself. Your pupils will love having pieces and exercises written especially for them!

**Chapter 4**
Motivation

## Early burn-out

It is worth noting that some pupils, at the age of seven or eight, have already been learning for possibly five years or more. To pre-empt early 'burn-out', the teacher must always be monitoring each pupil's level of enthusiasm, willingness to practise and to take part in musical activities. If enthusiasm does seem to be declining it is important to find out why. Usually the answer can be found out by careful questioning. To elicit truthful responses avoid direct questions. 'Which pieces do you enjoy playing most?' is better than 'Do you like the pieces you are learning?'. The former may lead to a particularly favoured style or indeed the answer 'None!' while the latter may simply draw a blanket 'They're okay', which tells you very little. If you ask leading questions, you will probably get the reply children think you want. If you ask questions that stimulate conversation, you will undoubtedly learn much more.

Perhaps the lesson may be on a day and at a time the child would very much rather be doing something else. It is also possible that the instrument may not be the right one: there may be physical problems that are causing frustration, the child may simply not like the sound their chosen instrument makes, or perhaps the repertoire may not be appropriate to the child's particular interests and tastes. Discussion between child, parent and teacher will often get to the root of the problem. Music can become such a joy in life that every effort must be made to protect it at this stage.

## The developing child

Of the many changes affecting children between 9 and 12 years of age, perhaps those most relevant to the music teacher are the development of a social life outside the home and the strength of peer-group pressure. This peer-group pressure can be so strong at times as to deter pupils from practising and may even cause them to give up.

For all beginners in this age group, it is important to choose your teaching materials with imagination. Children of 10 and 11 years of age have quite sophisticated tastes and would feel uneasy with many of the methods that are aimed at younger children. Players of wind and brass instruments often begin tuition about this time, and for these, owing to their physical development and learning experiences to date, it is a time of fairly rapid progress. Both beginners and well-established players should be encouraged to take part in social music-making activities. Suggest they join bands, orchestras or smaller groups as soon as they are able. Pianists can play duets or accompany friends. As well as being fun, it will put their music into a practical context.

Group dynamics may have a very positive effect on the older pupil's motivation. If geographical and time conditions are favourable, perhaps you can appoint your older pupils as mentors to your young beginners. Working on a one-to-one basis, the older pupil will enjoy a sense of responsibility; perhaps they will help with practice or assist in sorting out some technical problem. They can play duets and generally give the younger child a role model to look up to. Include the occasional group lesson in your programme (perhaps with a tea party to round off the event). Your pupils will enjoy being part of a group and can be taught to listen intelligently to their peers, comment constructively, and interact with you on a social level.

If a pupil is determined to give up, then there is not much you can do. There is no point insisting someone continues against their will, and while they may well regret it in future years, to continue will only produce frustration and bad feeling all round. Nevertheless, pupils should not be allowed to give up without some investigation. Perhaps a pianist merely finds the whole process too solitary: taking up the flute or trumpet, with the promise of speedy progress and a place in the school orchestra, may change their mind. Perhaps a clarinet player has always wanted to play jazz; although they may require a change of teacher, that is better than just allowing music to fade out for that individual. Perhaps the clarinettist's teacher does not play the piano, thus limiting the pupil to playing basic solo material that may be dull and uninspiring. Finding a friend who plays the piano well enough to manage simple accompaniments may well make the world of difference.

A recent survey by the Associated Board has identified a range of reasons why pupils give up. In addition to those already mentioned, some pupils find music begins to take up too much time, some were found not to like their teacher, others found that alternative hobbies began to become more prominent and time consuming, while in some cases the expense or technical challenges became too great. Interestingly enough the survey discovered that the greatest number of pupils gave up simply because they became *bored*. Finding out precisely why a pupil wishes to discontinue lessons may well yield a positive solution and you might be able to persuade a promising pupil not to give up after all.

## Adolescence

Adolescence constitutes the greatest challenge for pupil, teacher and parent. It is a time when life-energy is most focused and it is a period of instability. But it need not be a negative time, a period of 'storm and stress'; if the energy is seized and put to positive effect, the results can be very constructive. Self-esteem, which is often at a low level during adolescence, can be heightened by personal achievement and by contributing to activities that are both fun and artistically worthwhile.

The classic features of adolescence are well known to all teachers. Adolescents are self-conscious, strongly conform to peer-groups, are awakening to sex, concerned about physical appearance, and are becoming more independent. The degree to which adolescence affects different young people is marked: some are continually moody and find it difficult to focus on work; for others, adolescence seems almost to pass them by.

During some research carried out recently, a significant number of adults were asked what appealed most and what appealed least in their teachers throughout their own adolescence.

Characteristics most appreciated by pupils:
- giving pupils a sense of purpose;
- helping them to realize their ideals;
- stimulating pupils' ambition;
- inspiring self-confidence;
- taking an interest and showing kindness;
- possessing integrity, independence and energy.

Characteristics least appreciated by pupils:
- sarcasm;
- severity;
- absence of laughter and smiling;
- indifference.

When dealing with adolescents we might learn a lot from this list. In addition, it is often productive to take no notice of sullen behaviour but simply to carry on with business as usual. Pupils are apt to get annoyed if you draw attention to their unco-operative behaviour. Nevertheless, it may ultimately help them to 'snap out of it' if you do so in a light-hearted manner! Of course, in dealing with adolescents, a sense of humour is essential.

Young musicians in this age range will probably fall into one of the following groups:

**Those who have been playing for (many) years** They may be well motivated, enjoy lessons and other musical activities and see music as an important part of life, but not as a future career. Such pupils can, and should, be encouraged to reach very high levels of playing. They will find many opportunities available for playing at university or college and will continue to derive pleasure from music all through their lives.

**Those who have also been playing for (many) years but are now thinking this may be the time to give up** It is important to discuss the situation. If a decision to terminate lessons is made, it must be the result of careful consideration. As mentioned already there may be other factors to be taken into account which could alter the situation. These may be summarized as:

- Music may be too solitary: provision must be found to make it more social.
- Too much is expected, given the number of other commitments (both academic and social). A lightening of the load may be necessary for a time.
- The teacher (most probably through no fault of their own) may not be the right one for a particular pupil. A different teacher may offer a new angle.
- The pupil is not enjoying the kind of music they are being taught.
- The pupil needs a change of emphasis – a move away from an exam-centred programme for example.

Talk these issues through; you may find a way to resolve the situation without the pupil giving up their music. Some young players may be inspired by music technology. Many homes own a computer, and music software is both interesting and stimulating. The reluctant players may find a real interest in composing music to play on their own or with friends. They might enjoy sequencing or arranging music, or they might find the various interactive CD Roms provide a fun reason to practise!

**Those who have always enjoyed music, perhaps have sung in a choir and, with their new-found maturity, would now like to take up an instrument** Such musicians will be strongly motivated and, once they have got to grips with problems of technique and co-ordination (which will probably take some time to master), they will make good progress.

**Those who feel that music is going to become a career** This will be dealt with in Chapter 19.

> **Chapter 19**
> What Next?

## Teaching adults

Though the methods and strategies for teaching adults will be, broadly speaking, similar to those you use for teaching children, there will be some fundamental differences. Adults will be highly motivated but, at the same time, often dismissive of their ability. They also tend to be very critical of their achievements and will therefore require constant encouragement and reassurance. They will often say 'I know' when in fact they may not – reinforcement and repetition is therefore crucial. They will want to talk a lot and discuss technical and musical points much more than children do, and they will probably know quite a lot about music. Occasionally, you may have to be a little firm with those adults who question *everything* you say, or whose awkward manner begins to disturb the effectiveness of your teaching.

Clearly, the materials you use will need to be carefully chosen, but there are a number of methods now available especially written for the adult beginner. Adults may well not progress technically as fast as they would like, so choose music that is stimulating and rewarding to play. Encourage improvisation. Enter adults for exams only if they are determined and confident – they tend to be much more nervous than children. Adults may like to enter for the ABRSM Performance Assessment – a much more gentle and informal experience with no pass or fail.

# Chapter 3

# Lessons

## Evolving a curriculum

To many instrumental teachers the idea of 'evolving a curriculum' will probably seem unnecessary, unimportant or even somewhat intimidating! Effective instrumental teaching, however, does require both structure and direction and even though this may be uncharted territory for many, there is much to be said for thought and exploration in this subject.

Since very few countries prescribe any specific national syllabus for the learning of musical instruments, instrumental teachers are left to create their own. Many teachers fall into a kind of 'making it up as they go along' approach, the success of which depends largely on luck! So, as an efficient and thoughtful teacher, you will need to evolve, at least in general terms, your own 'curriculum'. It is not a complicated or daunting task, and your ideas will develop as you experiment, experience, explore and discover. This basic curriculum need not include anything more than:
- the methodical presentation of technique;
- knowing what repertoire you will use;
- the development of musicianship skills, including aural and sight-reading;
- appropriate suggestions for involving your pupils in musical activities outside the lesson.

As a result, the effectiveness of your teaching will almost certainly be noticeably enhanced.

Certain questions need to be considered. For beginners, should you base your teaching on a particular tutor book or method, or possibly a combination of methods? Should you use different methods for different pupils? Should you evolve your own method? And as your pupils progress, should you structure your teaching around grade exams?

Whichever avenue you choose, and it will probably be a combination of all the above, always bear in mind both the short-term and longer-term aims of your curriculum, and always explain them to, and discuss them with, your pupils. Young instrumentalists will greatly appreciate knowing both the rationale behind what you are teaching them and how this fits into their longer-term development.

## Teaching style

Just as the arts have been subjected to periods of considerable experimentation during the last hundred years, so too has music education. Instrumental teaching can now follow any path between the strict, no-nonsense, common-sense guidance given, for example, by Mrs Curwen in her *Pianoforte Method* (1886), and the more recent liberal methods, as formulated by music educators such as R. Murray Schafer and others. Here are some strategies taken from the writings of the above-mentioned teachers. Compare the two approaches:

**Mrs Curwen**
- Teach the easy before the difficult.
- Teach the thing before the sign.
- Teach one fact at a time.
- Proceed from the known to the related unknown.
- Let each lesson, as far as possible, arise out of that which goes before, and lead up to that which follows.
- Never tell pupils anything you can help them discover for themselves.

**R. Murray Schafer**
- Teach on the verge of peril.
- There are no more teachers. There is just a community of learners.
- The old approach: teacher has information; student has empty head. Teacher's objective: to push information into student's empty head. Observations: at outset teacher is a fathead; at conclusion student is a fathead.
- A class should be an hour of a thousand discoveries.
- Always teach provisionally: only God knows for sure.

In the typical one-to-one or small-group teaching that forms the heart of most instrumental teachers' work it would seem that Mrs Curwen's ideas are still, in the main, relevant, well over a hundred years after they were written. There is, nevertheless, much to be learned from Murray Schafer's broader and less prescriptive approach; perhaps most important is the necessity to remain flexible, open-minded and imaginative – qualities that are inherent in both approaches.

Your own teaching style will most likely be dependent, in part anyway, on knowledge gained from experience – from your own teachers, books you have read and ideas and techniques you have assimilated. Whether you are a traditional or a more 'modern' teacher, it is useful to give some thought to your own general approach. Currently, there is much discussion in educational circles concerning the relative merits of 'pro-active' versus 're-active' teaching. Imaginative teachers will find an appropriate balance that includes both these styles. Each pupil will require a slightly different approach, and the influences on any lesson are many – you need to be sensitive enough to adopt a flexible style of teaching at all times.

> **Chapter 11**
> Simultaneous Learning

## Learning styles

Imagine you have just bought yourself your first state-of-the-art computer. It is a very complicated machine. When you get it home, which of the following would your instinct lead you to do?
- Open the manual and read it thoroughly before switching on.
- Phone up a friend who has got the same machine and ask them to come round and teach you how to use it.
- Switch on and work it out through trial and error.

In fact, you would probably learn to operate your computer over a period of time using a combination of the above. Nevertheless, one of those methods is probably more dominant than the others. Reflect for a moment on whether you think your own preferred learning style influences your teaching style.

Your pupils will also have their own instinctive preference. Some will be punctilious, will want to read their tutors carefully and will instinctively learn in an intellectual and methodical kind of way. Some will depend very much on you and your guidance and show little of their own initiative. And some will want to try everything out, play a lot by ear and generally want to learn in a more creative kind of way.

It is useful to try to work out which learning style each pupil favours. It could have a beneficial effect both on your approach in lessons and on how you expect your pupils to approach their practice. Effective learners will draw on each of these learning styles and you should encourage your pupils to develop the learning styles that come less naturally to them.

## Basic principles of teaching

The following suggestions provide a summary of effective teaching practice. They represent a 'basic philosophy' that successful teachers adhere to, even without conscious analysis of their own methods. It is impossible to be entirely comprehensive and you may be able to add further thoughts; it is really a matter of common sense.

> - Understand clearly in your own mind what it is you intend to teach and what you expect your pupil to learn. A little forward planning goes a long way!
> - Make your explanations clear; use language, analogies and illustrations appropriate to the age (and interests) of your pupils. Be

Chapter 3

> prepared to explain the same problem in a number of different ways.
> - Make sure everything you teach is relevant and progressive.
> - Teach one thing at a time and ensure that it is understood before proceeding.
> - Ensure pupils have sufficient strategies for constructive and independent practice.
> - Revisit and reinforce new material (a weak link in the chain, which you may not notice at first, may come back to haunt both you and your pupil in the future).
> - Always set manageable goals but never be afraid to challenge your pupils.
> - Divide tasks into smaller manageable units if pupils are experiencing difficulties.
> - Clarification of some musical or technical point may be attained more easily through demonstration rather than verbal explanation.
> - Proceed from the known to the related unknown.
> - Use your pupil's existing knowledge, skills and experience to make connections to new ideas.
> - Always try to relate theory and aural to the particular repertoire being studied.

*... H.C. Robbins Landon writes that Haydn's symphony no. 28 in A opens with a movement which sounds like 6/8 for the first few bars but is actually in 3/4. The whole movement is ...*

## Lesson presentation

The actual lesson constitutes the main, and often the only, point of contact with the pupil. Care, thought and planning should therefore go into both its content and presentation. Ideally, pupils should always leave their lessons feeling positive about themselves, about what they have achieved and about what they are to practise. This will arise from an approach that is challenging, absorbing, rewarding, stimulating and methodical.

In his book *Common Sense in Music Teaching* William Lovelock states, 'Lessons have a twofold purpose: instruction and criticism'. He goes on to amplify both these terms: the former includes, for example, the broadening of the pupil's mind, and the latter, the giving of praise. Although he has indeed provided a pithy point of departure, it is necessary to delve much deeper to discover the secrets of presenting successful lessons and encouraging responsive and hard-working behaviour in pupils.

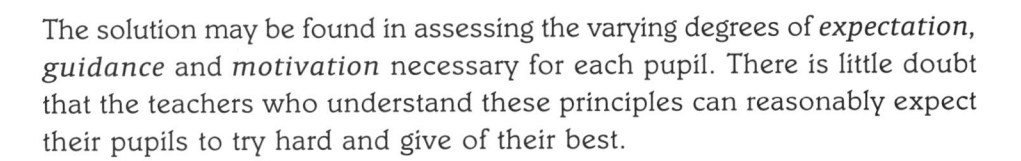

**Further Reading and References**

The solution may be found in assessing the varying degrees of *expectation*, *guidance* and *motivation* necessary for each pupil. There is little doubt that the teachers who understand these principles can reasonably expect their pupils to try hard and give of their best.

On entering the teaching room, the pupil should be greeted in a friendly and warm manner. Some discussion, be it topical, musical or connected perhaps with the pupil's academic, family or social life, will serve to set up a good rapport and indicate that you are taking an interest in them *as a person*. Try to establish and maintain an atmosphere of vigour; each teacher/pupil team will inevitably move at a different pace, but ensure that the forward impetus of the lesson is never lost.

### Expectation

Once the lesson 'proper' has begun, always expect the best from your pupil. Work set for practice should have been well prepared and you should always try to hear as much as time will allow. It is important that you keep your own record of exactly what you did set each pupil; the loss of a notebook can never then be an excuse, and pupils will soon come to realize that they will not get away with inefficient practice. Do not be afraid to 'tick off' a pupil if their practice is not up to your expectations. Pupils will often be testing you to see 'how much they can get away with' – make your expectations clear and, unless there is a good reason for poor practice, you should be annoyed. Make it apparent that you are annoyed because they are not working and thus not progressing – it must never be a personal attack! You can always find a way of getting annoyed sympathetically. Occasionally, a pupil *should* leave their lesson feeling that they were inadequately prepared or that they must work harder during the lesson. This is no bad thing.

During the lesson there should be periods both of intense concentration and shorter ones of relaxation; these will probably be determined by the length and content of the lesson. You may, for example, work up to your main focus of the lesson – some area of technique or a particular passage in a piece – then a short break, then a further intensive period of study and a final winding down when you will set practice work for the next lesson. Each individual has their own concentration span, which you will probably be able to ascertain after a few lessons; this will help you pace your lessons.

Encourage dialogue. Pupils should feel that you welcome the asking of intelligent questions – or you might promote some discussion over a technical or musical point. This will also assist you in finding the right pace for each pupil. Again, ask questions – find out whether enough time was spent on each topic (by you, the teacher) to cover it adequately.

**Guidance**

The second element is concerned with guiding pupils through the learning processes. In other words, what and how we actually teach. It is essential to teach methodically, moving from one point to another only when the first is fully understood. Watch carefully for a glazed look in the eye, or the lapsing of concentration; this is probably not the result of boredom or lack of interest, but of a lack of understanding through not paying sufficient attention to what you are saying (or perhaps because your explanation was not appropriate to that particular pupil). Equally, your pupil may be day dreaming or simply not bothering to say if they do not understand something. Again, establish the kind of dialogue that will allow the appropriate feedback – 'now describe that back to me in your own words' for example, or, perhaps, 'now you teach me how to do that'.

As for the detailed content and balance of a lesson, each teacher will have their own ideas, based on experience, tailored to fit the requirements of each pupil. Suffice it to say that variety is the spice of a good lesson and there should be both consolidation of recently learnt material and the introduction of new material. Don't feel that it is always necessary to dot all the i's and cross every t – brighter pupils will pick up ideas very quickly and, once recognized, this will save you a lot of time. Try to get your pupil to solve musical and technical problems by steering their thoughts in the right direction rather than simply telling them what to do.

Similarly, some pupils will require more motivating than others. This complex and important subject will be dealt with separately in Chapter 4.

## Lesson content

Most lessons will contain some combination of the four essential ingredients of instrumental learning:

- **Teaching specific musical skills,** such as instrumental or vocal technique; the development of musicianship through interpretative skills; aural training, sight-reading, memorizing, improvising and performance skills.
- **Imparting musical knowledge,** which will include explanations of musical vocabulary, technical concepts, theory and harmony as appropriate and even some history – musical, stylistic and instrument-specific.
- **Studying repertoire**
- **Performance practice**

You will rarely have time to cover everything in each lesson. You could, for example, focus on just one of these areas, but always bear in mind that musical skills cannot be compartmentalized so it is important to find methods of combining the various strands of musical learning where possible. If you do structure your lessons in the same way as an exam (pieces, scales and technical work, sight-reading and aural), take care to vary the order. Avoid always beginning your lessons with pieces for example; instead begin with sight-reading or aural. It is also important to end lessons on a positive note – the playing of a favourite piece or some 'fun' sight-reading for example.

**Chapter 11** ➤
Simultaneous Learning

## The first lessons

The content and presentation of the first lesson is of considerable importance – if you plan nothing else, you should plan this! As always, first impressions are very important. The image you present when you first meet a new pupil should be kind, calm, efficient and methodical.

If you have not already met your new pupil, the first lesson will be something of a 'voyage of discovery'. You will need to appraise both their personality and musicianship, but this should be done subtly. Your new pupil will probably be nervous and wary; you should therefore do your best to avoid intimidating or 'putting them on the spot' in any way. Make it an enjoyable and friendly experience. Find out what they would like to achieve from their lessons and agree on realistic objectives. (For example 'I want to play jazz like Stefan Grapelli by Christmas' is probably not a likely prospect; 'I want to be able to play/improvise simple pieces and sound good' is more within the realms of possibility!) By the end of the lesson their basic personality will have emerged and this will help you determine the type of approach necessary – for example, the sort of repertoire you will use, the pace of your teaching and the attitude you will adopt.

You may like to give some simple aural tests to provide a basic indication of your pupil's musicianship but, again, be careful to avoid upset or embarrassment. If you are taking on a more advanced pupil you will probably use the time to hear them play a recently learned piece and discuss their musical (and other) interests and aspirations. Take great care when discussing their previous teacher: try not to criticize, undermine or attack the quality of the teaching (even if you feel outraged by what you find). It is unprofessional and may be taken personally and thus seriously upset your new pupil.

The remaining time should be spent laying down some basic ground rules: what you want to be called, how much practice you expect and so on. It's easy to relax your expectation at certain psychologically appropriate moments in the future, but much more difficult to get tougher! Make sure that all you teach in the first lesson is very clearly understood and that your pupil knows exactly what you expect them to practise. You will most likely include some work on posture, sound production and possibly some introduction to rhythm and notation. Don't forget that pupils will probably be very enthusiastic and eager to learn – make good use of this!

The period between the first two lessons is also crucial. It is the time to decide on repertoire and basic strategies. Avoid using the same material for each beginner. Try to wait until after the first lesson to make your decisions – there are so many different methods available, each with their own particular slant, and the careful and conscientious teacher will wish to find the most appropriate. Varying your teaching material will also help you to avoid slipping into a kind of 'auto-pilot' mode. Your own involvement in the teaching material is essential if you are to fire the imagination of your pupil.

Be sure to expect practice to have been thoroughly prepared and set high standards of playing and attitude in these early lessons; it will pay great dividends in the future.

You may find that a parent wishes to 'sit in' during the first lessons (or indeed subsequent lessons). Some teaching methods (the Suzuki method for example) encourage this most strongly, with the parent being taught almost as much as the child, so that there is always help at hand during the early stages of practice and development. Many non-Suzuki teachers will similarly see considerable benefits in having a parent present (although it should be made clear that the visitor should remain a *silent* onlooker). Musical parents, for example, might be encouraged to take notes throughout the lesson, saving you valuable time otherwise spent filling out your pupil's notebook. However comprehensive you manage to make your notes, much will probably be forgotten (by your younger pupils) or wilfully ignored (by your older ones!); thus, this kind of parental help may be invaluable in supporting your work and causing progress to be made much more quickly. Other teachers may not feel comfortable teaching to an audience; if you fall into this group, it is important to ask yourself why. Whichever way you do finally decide to deal with this matter, parents should respect your point of view unquestioningly.

## Lesson etiquette

The following points look at what we might term 'lesson etiquette'. It is not suggested that you try to implement them either as a 'package' or in an excessively demanding way, but rather that you take from them what you consider suitable for each pupil. Lessons must never be tense and there must always be room for humour and laughter. It is no bad thing, however, to impress upon your pupils that you take the matter of teaching and lessons seriously. You will have to adjust and adapt for different age ranges but they will form a basic set of rules that you can deviate from or adhere to as necessary.

- Do not accept poor preparation.
- Expect pupils to come to lessons clean, tidy and alert.
- They should learn to get their music (and instrument) ready quickly and without fuss.
- Check that all music required and notebook are brought to lessons (a minor penalty for forgetting may help to jog the memory on future occasions!).
- Make sure pupils know to tell you immediately if they do not understand something.
- Ask for regular feedback.
- Expect an appropriate response time to instruction.
- Maintain eye contact during instruction – do not let a pupil's eyes wander around the room.
- Do not accept negative body language – keep a watchful eye on facial expression and posture and gently pull pupils up for sending out negative signals. The whole question of motivating pupils is dealt with in the next chapter.

**Chapter 4**

Motivation

# Chapter 4

# Motivation

It is always a pleasure when your pupils enter your lesson smiling broadly, alert, responsive and having done all their practice. Unfortunately, this is not always the case. For those less-than-model pupils, understanding them and knowing how to motivate them is an essential part of teaching.

## Defining motivation

Some years ago a group of American educational psychologists conducted experiments to discover the main components involved in bringing about academic achievement. They found these to be intelligence, personality, social variables and motivation. Interestingly enough, for most school subjects, they found that all four had about equal effect. Because motivation plays an important part in successful teaching and learning, it is of considerable importance to know how to maintain a good level of motivation and whether it is possible to influence the level of motivation.

The dictionary definition of motivation is 'that which causes a person to act in a certain way'. However, it is necessary to take our investigation a little further and to recognize that there are a number of 'layers' involved in an individual's motivation, not all of which may be experienced by the less-motivated pupil. These may be identified as follows:

- **Layer 1** – The nature of the activity itself. This may be interpreted in a broad context (for example, wanting to play the piano), or it may be more specific (for example, wanting to learn a particular piece of music they have heard).
- **Layer 2** – The intensity of interest the individual has in the activity.
- **Layer 3** – A recognition by the pupil of the consequences and advantages of undertaking the activity.

Thus, a specific pupil-model might be:
- **Layer 1** – I want to learn the piano.
- **Layer 2** – I want to learn the piano very much.

- **Layer 3** – I want to learn the piano very much because of the great pleasure it will afford me/my parents/friends; I want to show the world what I can do; I would like to accompany my friend; I would like to play Christmas carols and so on.

Having some idea of where pupils sit in relation to these motivational layers is both useful and revealing. Not all pupils, for example, will have developed Layer 3; in other words, although they might have a strong desire to learn, they might not be able to articulate *why* they want to do so. An understanding of the strength and direction of their motivation may well help you in understanding and dealing with their highs and lows.

## Motivation in practice

Learning to play a musical instrument is normally the result of choice. Ideally, taking up an instrument should have been the pupil's choice, and in such cases the particular individual will already possess a fundamental desire to develop their abilities (in other words, be a well-motivated pupil). More often than not, though, it will have been the choice of the parent. It is for these pupils that a knowledge and understanding of their motivation becomes particularly useful.

We might say that signs of a highly motivated pupil are enthusiasm, efficient practising and a receptive, positive disposition throughout lessons. Only rarely is this the case on all counts. For most pupils, the degree of motivation, particularly when affected by the moods of adolescence, will fluctuate. Can we, therefore, find a way to monitor a pupil's motivation and increase or supplement it if necessary? There are certainly a number of factors that can be kept under careful scrutiny.

*Chapter 2 — Age and Approach*

> Try asking yourself the following questions in relation to those pupils whose motivation you might question:
> - Is practice regular, efficient and effective?
> - Is behaviour positive at lessons?
> - Is there a ready, thoughtful and intelligent response to your comments?
> - Is trouble taken over correct posture?
> - Are music and notebook always brought to lessons?
> - Is their instrument being looked after?
> - Is there enthusiasm for taking part in associated musical activities?
> - Does the pupil ever undertake extra work they have not been set by you?

If the answer to the majority (or at least some) of these questions is 'yes', then you have a reasonably well-motivated pupil. What can be done for those pupils who are less motivated? First of all your general attitude to the pupil, and the manner in which you present new material, should be considered. Do you look forward to each pupil's lesson? If not, you need to ask yourself why. New material is best introduced imaginatively, positively and as part of an on-going, developing, learning process. A negative approach is much less successful: 'You've got to learn these scales or you won't pass your exam', will not inspire a positive attitude (even if exam passing is the prime motivator!). Is each pupil enjoying the majority of the work you are setting them?

You must be enthusiastic and encouraging, although you should have it in you to put your foot down if the need arises – your pupil must sense this even if you never actually do it! Never underestimate the power of praise: praise your pupils frequently. All teachers acknowledge the importance of praising the beginner every step of the way, but praise, when it is appropriate, should be no less forthcoming for the more advanced student.

As you get to know a pupil you will begin to be able to identify special interests and enthusiasms. You may like to use these as rewards: once some difficult technical problem has been overcome you could, for example, reward it with a piece by a favoured composer or a lesson of duets or whatever your pupil especially enjoys.

Most students will benefit from taking part in regular musical activities. These are ideal ways of focusing and directing work and will, in most cases, act as powerful sources of motivation. In addition, participating in ensembles, bands, orchestras or choirs will allow young players to mix with others who have similar interests.

**Chapter 2**
Age and Approach

Pupils will often work best when there is a goal in sight: a performance at a concert or music festival or an exam. You might like to set up your own inter-pupil competitions – an end-of-term scales competition, for example, can be surprisingly successful! Young people, in general, enjoy competition, and with the prize of a large bar of chocolate (or a scale book!) this type of unlikely event might be the highlight of a term.

**Chapter 16/17**
Examinations/ Competitions and Festivals

**Chapter 8**
Teaching Scales

Pianists could be teamed up to accompany friends who play other instruments and, for the more serious pupil, they could be encouraged to attend music courses, or to 'mentor' a younger pupil. Some pupils respond well to regular assessment – at the end of lessons you may like to give each pupil a grade (such as A, B or C) for Practice (how well they have prepared set work), Performance (the way they played during the lesson) and Progress (since the last lesson). The Lesson Plan/Record Sheet provided at the back of the book has space for just such an assessment.

**Chapter 2**
Age and Approach

Perhaps the overall golden rule in maintaining motivation is that your expectations should always be very clear and appropriate to the particular

Lesson Plan/ Record Sheet

pupil. The correct balance of new and challenging work, together with the revisiting and reinforcing of old and previously prepared work, should maintain a healthy level of motivation. If the expectation is too little, pupils will get bored, and, if too great, they may become daunted and lose interest. Expectation may also be perceived as the relationship between a pupil's ability and potential. The greater a pupil's potential, the greater the demands you can make. The important factor is that pupils are always realistically challenged at their own level so that they are always likely to achieve, and thus progress, at their optimum rate.

Always make sure that pupils complete tasks, and complete them to the best of their ability. This will lead to confidence, which in turn will motivate them towards the next challenge. Here is the ideal motivational model:

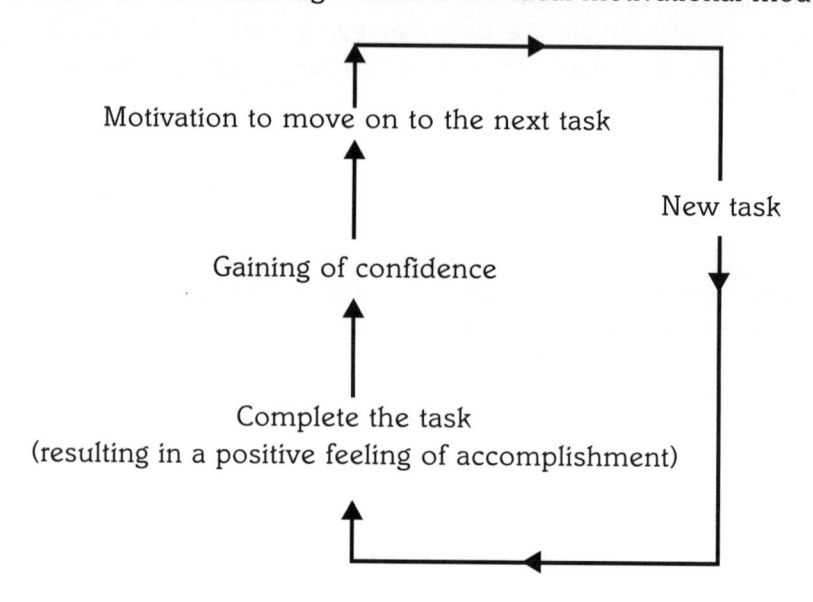

```
     ┌──────────────────────────────────────┐
     ↓                                      │
Motivation to move on to the next task      │
     ↑                                      │
     │                                  New task
Gaining of confidence                       │
     ↑                                      │
     │                                      │
Complete the task                           │
(resulting in a positive feeling of accomplishment)
     ↑                                      │
     └──────────────────────────────────────┘
```

## Poor motivation

There may still be pupils who are continually sullen and uninterested and who do not respond to any of your motivational endeavours; such pupils may perhaps best be recommended to give up or change instruments or come back to music at a later time. Do not be afraid to take this course of action, since time and money may otherwise be spent with no positive benefit.

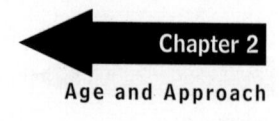

Occasionally, pupils may become poorly motivated for practical or personal reasons. An instrument that is not functioning properly, for example, may well be a source of frustration. Pupils can suffer from particularly over-zealous parents or be intimidated by peers who tease them for practising rather than socialising. If you notice a sudden drop in motivation, try to 'go behind the scenes' for an explanation: speak with a class teacher or tutor, a parent or guardian, possibly a friend – someone who might be able to shed light on the situation. If you suspect that the problem may be serious, avoid confrontation or even discussion until you have some idea of what it might be. If you feel it is within your remit, then discussion may provide a way forward. If the problem is one you do not feel equipped to take on, then you should probably alert the appropriate professional body. In these kinds of instance it is of some importance to have at least a working knowledge of any appropriate legislation concerning dealings with young people.

## Transferring responsibility as a form of motivation

From time to time, instead of you setting the shape and content of the lesson, transfer that responsibility to your pupil. Begin the lesson by asking what *they* would like to do: 'Which piece would you like to work on?' 'Which sections need help?'. You might ask them to prepare their whole lesson before they come, and to write down exactly what they would like included. Question any omissions – no scales for example. Are they not keen to improve their technique?

You will find that handing over responsibility in this way may have a very positive effect on both well-motivated and less-motivated pupils. It will also cause them to think about their work from a different and useful angle, focusing their own thoughts on areas of weakness. Similarly, it will improve the efficiency of their practice by causing them to identify the problems requiring most attention.

# Monitoring Your Work

Monitoring your work is an important issue for all teachers, and particularly for the instrumental teacher, who may work in isolation both from other teachers and from other aspects of the pupil's learning processes. Such isolation necessitates a rigorous approach to self-evaluation.

It is all too easy to rely on familiar and comparative yardsticks and to let them become a substitute for 'active' monitoring. For example, the teacher who uses the same tutor book or pieces repeatedly may be inclined to measure the progress of one pupil against his or her peers, rather than against the individual's real capabilities or potential. In this way, difficulties or shortcomings may be overlooked, or rapid progress may be hindered by a failure to match the teaching material with the learning requirements. If you do use one tutor book regularly, avoid comparing one pupil's progress with that of another. There is very little more dispiriting for one pupil to be told that another 'reached Stage 3 in two weeks and it's taken you 25!'

Effective monitoring requires vigour and objectivity. An effective way to begin your own monitoring process is to use either audio or video recording. With the agreement of your pupil, record one or two lessons and then sit back, observe and analyze your performance!

There are a number of areas to consider.

## Language — praise and criticism

The language you use and the manner in which you say things are very significant and may indeed be a crucial factor in the success of your teaching. Make a note of the positive and negative comments made. Remember that there is always more than one way to say the same thing; the following examples may help:

| **Positive comments** | **Negative comments** |
|---|---|
| Well done, you produced a good tone, but I wonder whether we can work on . . . | The tone is still not good enough. |
| I enjoyed the phrasing here, but we need to hear it throughout the piece . . . | Is that phrasing the best you can do? Why do you ignore phrasing in this section? |
| Good, you remembered this F sharp, but what about the rest? | But what about the F sharps? |
| You have remembered some of the things we talked about last lesson, but how did you get on with . . . | You must practise more. |
| The articulation is so much better than last week, but I still think you could do more . . . | The articulation still isn't clear. |
| You started with much better posture, but . . . | You still haven't sorted out your posture. |
| That is beginning to communicate a real sense of performance, but we need to hear more . . . | It's still not very expressive. |
| Let's do some more work on rhythm. | Don't you know the difference between a crotchet and a quaver yet? |

## Language – technical terms

How many technical, musical or Italian terms are you using during the course of a lesson? Does your pupil seem to understand them? How often do you ask pupils to explain them to you? These words and expressions are important in enabling pupils to operate efficiently in teaching and rehearsing situations, so any gaps in their knowledge may have serious 'knock-on' effects.

## Planning and preparation

**→ Lesson Plan/Record Sheet**

Monitoring presupposes that each lesson has undergone some planning and preparation. By using the Lesson Plan/Record Sheets you will be able to note whether the work you intended to do has been covered. Take a few seconds to fill in these forms. They will help to remind you exactly where you are with each pupil and will be a useful way of monitoring your pupil's work and progress. The evaluation boxes can be filled in with a grade (A – C, or whatever you feel appropriate). A lesson might move in a direction quite different from that originally intended, but this does not necessarily diminish its value – it may well add to it!

**→ Termly Overview Sheet**

The Termly Overview Sheets are very useful to help you plan each term; they also act as a constructive template for an end-of-term review. You may wish to use them as a form of report.

## Music and general content

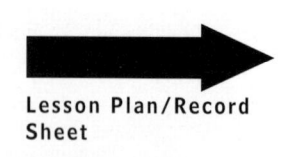

Over a period of, say, ten lessons make a note (for each pupil) of the general balance of content: the number of pieces played, the number of scales learnt, the number of times you included aural, sight-reading, improvisation and other areas of musicianship. How well-balanced a diet do you feel each pupil is getting?

Many instrumental teachers measure success by whether or not they retain pupils, by exam and festival successes and by the existence of a waiting list of children wanting to have lessons with them. These are important, but equally important is for the teacher to develop skills as a reflective practitioner, always questioning the choice and effectiveness of materials and teaching strategies. In this way, long-term success is more likely, and a freshness of approach, which characterizes all good teaching, may be assured.

## Time for reflection . . .

### On a specific pupil

Occasionally, you might like to sit back and reflect on a particular pupil, especially if you feel all is perhaps not going as well as it might.

> Consider the following questions carefully:
> - How do you rate your pupil's general attitude to work set?
> - What are your feelings towards the pupil?
> - What are your feelings about what you are teaching the pupil?
> - How do you rate your ability to teach what the pupil is studying?
> - What is your perception of the pupil's progress?
> - What is your general frame of mind in relation to the pupil?

By reflecting in this way you may well identify particular areas of concern that can be improved on or dealt with by subtle changes in attitude or approach. In addition, if you are feeling anxious, under pressure, unhappy or under-confident, these emotions can sometimes be transferred on to your pupil (and, of course, *vice versa*). This is known as 'received feeling' by psychotherapists. It is as well to consider your state of mind at the beginning of a teaching session (particularly in the case of any 'problem' pupils) – it could have quite a significant effect on the success of that teaching.

### On a specific lesson

Even though instrumental and singing teachers tend to have extremely busy lives it is a good idea to sit back and reflect occasionally on a specific lesson.

> Ask yourself the following questions:
> - What were your main objectives?
> - What did you actually do?
> - Do you feel you achieved your objectives?
> - What contributed to the success (or otherwise) of the lesson?
> - Would you have done anything differently?

# Chapter 6 — Teaching Rhythm

# Teaching Rhythm

## What is rhythm?

Rhythm, in its broadest sense, is the subdivision of time into perceivable units. Together with melody and harmony it is one of the three basic elements of music, and all three are entirely interdependent: melody and harmony would have no movement without rhythm, and rhythm without melody and harmony is only of limited interest.

There are a number of commonly used terms in relation to rhythm, and there is much debate, confusion and difference of opinion among both musicians and even theorists as to what each of these terms actually means. The word 'rhythm' is used to describe all notational aspects of music as distinct from pitch, as well as having a more specific meaning (discussed below). The problem with understanding these terms is that many are interchangeable and often used in an imprecise way. As teachers we use these expressions on a regular basis and it is important that we have a clear idea in our own minds as to their function. Here, then, are some definitions that attempt to clarify their meaning, and also show how they are often used.

> Note down what you understand by each of the following terms:
> - pulse
> - beat
> - metre
> - rhythm
> - time
>
> Now compare your answers with the text below.

**Pulse** The division of time (in its non-musical sense) into (usually) regular units.

**Beat** The name given to each unit. For example, in $\frac{4}{4}$ each ♩ is one beat;

in $^6_8$ each ♩. is one beat. Also used in such directions as 'play on the beat', 'keep the beat steady', 'that piece had a good beat'.

**Metre**  The grouping of beats into patterns of strong and weak. For example, in $^3_4$ the metrical pattern is: strong – weak – weak. Metre establishes bars.

**Rhythm**  When we ask pupils to 'tap the rhythm of a melody' we expect them to tap the varying patterns of note lengths within each bar. When a performance is described as 'rhythmical', however, it implies more than an accurate rendition of the time values of the notes. There must also be a strong sense of both metre and pulse. Thus, rhythm can be defined as musical movement marked by a regular succession of strong or weak elements.

**Time**  The arrangement and number of beats in the bar. For example, simple duple time. Also used to denote the maintenance of a steady pulse in relation to tempo (playing 'in time').

Of these terms, metre is one that you will probably hardly ever use in a practical teaching situation. Nevertheless, it is useful to have a precise idea of this full 'sequence' of definitions; it is always the case that the more clearly a concept is understood the better it will be taught. Think through the ways that you use each of these terms, and, when appropriate, ask your pupils to explain to you what they understand by them.

## Have I got rhythm?

Some people seem to be born with a sense of rhythm, others not. For those that don't possess a natural sense of rhythm, learning to play or sing becomes much more of a challenge. But do they really lack a rhythmic sense? We all have a heartbeat, breathe, walk and do other 'rhythmic' activities during the course of our daily lives. The problem that concerns music teachers is that of accessing and then developing the pupil's (often well-hidden) rhythmic sense.

There are some basic 'tests' you can try, to find out whether pupils have an innate sense of rhythm.

> Ask your pupil to tap the pulse of a piece as you play it. Can they feel the metre (i.e. where the strong beat comes)? Can they tap this beat more strongly? Stop playing and see whether they can continue tapping the pulse steadily.
>
> Count a few bars out loud, then ask your pupil to continue counting in their heads. After ten or so bars of silent counting see whether you've both arrived on the same beat of the same bar. (When time

> permits try this over 20 or more bars; it is a very good exercise to develop the 'inner' metronome!)
>
> Begin playing a simple piece and count out loud for two bars: 1 2 3 4, 2 2 3 4. Ask your pupil to count in their heads. Stop counting aloud but continue playing. After a number of bars, stop suddenly and ask which bar (and possibly which beat) you stopped on.
>
> Begin tapping a steady pulse, about ♩ = 60. Ask your pupil to join in, tapping two quavers/eighth notes (or ask for two even or equal notes) to each pulse.
>
> Ask your pupil to sing you a song they know well – 'Happy Birthday' for example. You will recognize the rhythmical performer.
>
> Can your pupil tell whether two very simple rhythms are the same or different?

Many young children should be able to do fairly well in these tests, and you can further improve children's rhythmic sense simply with regular application of such tests – most pupils will find them rather fun! If there is a serious problem with rhythm, however, progress will always be slow and frustrating, but as long as the pupil is keen, and lots of time is devoted to the development of the rhythmic sense in the early stages of learning, progress will be made. If the pupil is not keen, or if taking up the instrument is entirely parentally motivated, it might be wise to recommend a change to a different interest!

## Teaching pulse

The prime intention here is to instil an 'inner metronome' – the ability to feel an ongoing steady pulse, one of the two essential skills necessary to underpin a secure sense of rhythm.

The Swiss composer and educationalist Emile Jaques-Dalcroze developed a method of music education based on rhythm, movement and aural training; it is known as Eurythmics. The method is not only suitable for young children – teachers can borrow and adapt the ideas for all age ranges. The method encourages pupils to develop their sense of pulse by experiencing it physically. The following is a 'Dalcroze-style' activity designed to co-ordinate mind and body in the development of pulse. Many Dalcroze activities require space for walking, marching, dancing or other kinds of movement. This one can be done in a reasonably confined space. You will need a ball!

> Play a piece of music with a clear pulse and metre; it is advisable to begin with either two or four beats to the bar. Pupils bounce the ball in time to the music, giving an emphasis where they hear the strong pulse. When all is going smoothly change the time: try three and five beats in the bar.

Dalcroze was convinced that the pulse should always be physically felt, rather than mentally generated. Here is an exercise that may help identify whether the pulse is, as it were, incorrectly activated.

> Ask your pupil to tap a steady pulse (at a moderate tempo). Join in, tapping with the pulse, then introduce other rhythmic values (quavers/eighth notes, triplets, minims/half notes, for example). If the pupil finds it difficult to maintain the steady pulse, or the pulse becomes unsteady, it is probably because the pulse is mentally, rather than physically, propelled; the extra mental burden caused by your varied rhythms results in hesitancy. If there are problems, try some strongly physical activities: beating a pulse loudly on a drum, marching on the spot and so on.

With a little lateral thinking you will be able to design a whole host of similar activities that will help develop pupils' physical feeling for pulse. In addition, you can revisit some of the 'diagnostic' exercises outlined above.

## The vital importance of subdivision

Once pupils have grasped, or are beginning to grasp, a sense of pulse, they must learn to:
- subdivide the pulse;
- maintain a steady pulse whatever the subdivision.

The ability to understand and feel these subdivisions is the other essential part of learning to play rhythms accurately: only in this way will rhythmic security be assured.

Try the following exercises.

> Tap or clap a steady pulse. Ask your pupil to clap or tap along with you. Now ask them to *think* two beats to each pulse. After a while ask them to tap the two beats.
>
> Repeat the exercise, but this time ask for each pulse to be split into three.
>
> Ask your pupil to *think* a steady crotchet/quarter note pulse. After a while ask them to tap quavers/eighth notes, whilst still thinking the crotchet pulse.
>
> Tap or clap a slow steady pulse. Ask your pupil to clap or tap along with you. Now ask them to split the pulse into two, return to the pulse after a while, then split into three, return to the pulse, and then finally split into four
>
> Begin again as last time, but now ask for the two, three and four subdivisions in varying order, for example, into two, now four, now three, now four again, now two and so on.

Pupils can also sing or play the exercises. As you work at these musical 'rhythm games' you will find yourself thinking up new (and ever more sophisticated) permutations. Do this kind of work often, especially at the earlier stages of learning – it will reap great rewards.

For the more advanced pupil an immediate reaction to changing subdivisions is essential. Set up a fairly slow pulse and ask your pupil to join in. At irregular intervals, ask pupils to subdivide the pulse into two, three, four, five, six, seven or eight. When this becomes fluent and reliable you will know that a very useful skill has been assimilated. Another difficult, but very useful, exercise is to get pupils to tap a pulse with their foot, clap or tap one subdivision with their hands while counting a further subdivision out loud – all simultaneously! Here's a particularly testing example:

> Tap pulse with foot.
> Clap two to each pulse.
> Count aloud five to each pulse (or say 'hippopotamus'!).

This exercise can be taken one step further!

> Again, tap the pulse with the foot, then, on a table or flat surface, tap a different subdivision with each hand and count aloud a further subdivision!

The permutations are endless.

## Teaching rhythmic patterns

Once pupils have a sense of pulse and simple subdivision then the learning of rhythmic patterns will not be an insurmountable challenge. It is very important to choose your teaching material carefully in the early stages of learning. Rhythmic patterns should be introduced gradually; overloading at this time can be quite detrimental.

When introducing a new rhythm or rhythmic pattern try either the following sequence, or select some elements from it (or devise your own strategy along similar lines). Teachers who merely tell their pupils how rhythms 'go' are doing those pupils no favours. Rhythm must be taught thoroughly.

- Explain the rhythm and relate it to the pulse.
- Pupil taps the pulse while you tap the rhythm.
- Pupil taps the rhythm while you tap the pulse.
- Pupil thinks the pulse while you tap the rhythm.
- Pupil thinks the pulse and taps the rhythm.
- Pupil taps the rhythm and vocalizes the pulse – counting beats or simply saying 'Ta', 'Pom' (or any appropriate syllable) for each beat.
- Pupil sings the rhythm (to 'la' or any appropriate syllable) and taps the pulse.
- Pupil both taps and vocalizes the rhythm to 'Ta' or 'Pom' (or another syllable).
- Pupil taps the pulse with one hand and the rhythm with the other.
- Pupil repeats the above with hands reversed.

Once you get into the idea of these kinds of exercise more will come to mind. Those given above are progressive in difficulty; the co-ordination required becomes more complex. Only go as far as you can with each pupil. Pupils should be challenged but not given tasks that will leave them frustrated and demoralized. All pupils should be able to get as far as point 4; the succeeding exercises should then be introduced and developed gradually.

Remember also the importance of connecting the known to the unknown in the learning process. Complex rhythms can, for example, always be introduced by simplifying them first:

H. J. Baermann

A further aid to the teaching of rhythm are 'flash cards' (cards each printed with short rhythmic patterns, available from many music shops). You can devise all sorts of ways to combine them with the various teaching strategies suggested above.

**Word rhythms**
Younger pupils will probably have encountered relating words to rhythms in the classroom. For some, it may have a very beneficial effect in accelerating their learning. Find a simple way of expressing where they live, their favourite food, football team or whatever, in notated rhythm:

Pic-ca-dil-ly     Hud-ders-field     Car-diff     Man-ches-ter U- ni-ted

As you tap a pulse or play a simple series of, say, tonic and dominant chords on the piano, your pupil taps out their 'word(s)' at regular intervals. You can have a lot of fun using this technique in the group situation. Pupils will enjoy thinking up all sorts of familiar phrases that can be used to introduce a variety of rhythms. If you have time and are feeling adventurous your group could create 'minimalist' pieces (for example, in the style of Steve Reich!) using various simultaneous rhythmic ostinatos.

It is also useful approaching this idea from the other direction. Ask your pupil to think up words to an existing rhythmic pattern – perhaps part of a piece they find difficult to grasp.

## Teaching counting

Counting does not necessarily have anything to do with numbers; in essence it is the successful feeling of pulse. However, counting numbers, at least in the early stages of learning, is probably a good idea. As pupils are learning new rhythms and pieces (and if the instrument will allow) recommend that pupils count out aloud from time to time; they should count confidently and with real physical involvement – ONE! TWO! ONE! TWO! – so that the pulse is physically *felt*. This has the effect of putting both order and vitality into the pulse, thus instilling a secure foundation on which to attach the rhythmic patterns. Again, you can evolve various 'games' to develop this skill. For example:

> Tap the rhythm whilst counting the pulse (numbers) out loud.
> Tap the rhythm whilst counting the pulse in your head (loudly!).

**Chapter 7**
Teaching Sight-Reading

**When is 'one' not 'one'?**
There is a problem with music counting that represents real conceptual confusion for some pupils. In measuring distance, for example, when we reach the one-kilometre post we have travelled one kilometre; that point represents a whole unit, with the 'one' or '1' forming the end marker.

In music when we say 'one' we are indicating the *start* of the beat. Thus, when teaching 'music counting' we are turning a known concept on its head. Many pupils will understand this intuitively (in which case nothing need be said!), but for others it may need a certain degree of careful explanation. For example, those players who always cut long notes off short are often not thinking *through* beats; in other words they stop a note at the beginning of its final beat.

## Pulse and tempo

Within the context of teaching rhythm, it is the ability to react and adapt to a particular tempo and to feel the appropriate subdivisions that is fundamental.

Try the following exercises to help develop these responses:

> You are going to tap crotchets/quarter notes in $\frac{4}{4}$ time at a fairly slow pulse (♩ = 60). After a one-bar 'introduction' ask your pupil to tap quavers/eighth notes for two bars. In the next bar increase the tempo (to about ♩ = 80) and again ask your pupil to tap quavers/eighth notes for two bars. Continue the sequence, increasing the tempo to a limit of about ♩ = 144.
>
> Repeat as above but alternate between quavers/eighth notes and triplets. Make your tempo changes more dramatic and random.

Again, you will find yourself developing your own exercises.

How does one choose a tempo? The composer's markings and metronome indications (if given) will help, of course. Many musicians argue that every piece of music has its own natural tempo. Clearly, this is not so in any absolute sense; different performers seem (successfully) to bring a wide range of tempi to the same piece. What is important for young players is that they play in a variety of tempi, rather than play all their pieces in the same or a very similar tempo!

# Teaching Sight-Reading

## Why learn to sight-read?

Fluent sight-reading is arguably the most valuable skill for young musicians to acquire. There are, of course, a number of obvious benefits:
- Pupils will be able to learn new music more quickly.
- Good marks will be obtained in sight-reading tests.
- Pupils will become musically independent, allowing them to experience the many joys of music-making throughout their lives.

There is, in addition, an even more important reason for encouraging our pupils to become good sight-readers. In the normal course of a teaching day a considerable amount of time is spent simply correcting mistakes caused, mostly, by poor, insecure or lazy music-reading. The development of this skill will prevent valuable time being wasted on tedious note learning, and thus allow you to focus on the 'musical' essence of a piece.

## The reading process

There has been much scientific investigation into the processes we use to read. When reading text the eye makes very rapid short movements (called 'saccades'), followed by longer periods of 'fixations' during which the actual reading and processing of the text takes place. This sequence of movements occurs two or three times per second. The 'fixations' can take in anything from a letter or a short word to a phrase or even a sentence. Eye movements are generally forward, but there will also be backward (or regressive) movements to check over what has already been read. When reading music the eye makes similar movements, but some interesting differences have been observed. In reading music, the eye makes *more* movements than when reading text – five or six times per second is not unusual – and more regressive (backward) movements are common. In fact, the eye is scanning the music, including both horizontal and vertical movements, thus building up a kind of overall picture.

Although eye movement itself cannot be trained (good or bad eye movements are the result of reading habits and will not in themselves cause poor reading) an awareness of how the eye works can certainly be used to help increase efficiency.

## The basic elements of sight-reading

There are three basic elements involved in the sight-reading process:
- recognizing pitch;
- understanding rhythm;
- combining notes and rhythm whilst maintaining a steady pulse.

### Pitch

Seeing a note, knowing its name and translating this information into the appropriate set of physical movements needs to be a virtually instantaneous process. If you think your pupil lacks fluency in note-reading, use 'flash-cards' or write out a page of notes (in the appropriate range) for practice. Continue this kind of work until you feel your pupil has acquired the necessary fluency. Pupils should be taught to recognize note patterns as they do familiar words. From the earliest stages point out patterns that are based on scales or arpeggios, triads or chords, repeated melodic shapes, repeated accompaniment figures, and so on. Perhaps you might circle obvious patterns to encourage perception of these shapes and you might talk about the similarity with word-reading. We don't read words letter by letter, but take in words, phrases, sometimes even whole sentences, at a glance, and pupils will soon grasp that we read music in much the same way.

### Rhythm

In grade exams the majority of problems result not from faulty note-reading but rather from not playing the notes *in time*. So it is the teaching of pulse, rhythm and counting that is fundamental for the sight-reader, particularly in the early stages. Once you are convinced that your pupils can maintain a steady pulse, both physically (clapping or tapping for example) and 'internally' (counting in their heads), they must then learn to relate pulse to rhythm. It is essential that pupils understand rhythm if they are to achieve fluency in their sight-reading. You will therefore need to reinforce each new rhythmic pattern time after time until pupils recognize them and respond both accurately and immediately.

It is very important that pupils establish an internal pulse before sight-reading a piece. In the early stages you might ask them to count *four bars* before playing. This will help the development of a really stable pulse. Two bars should be counted out loud and then two silently; this has the advantage of allowing you to hear whether their counting is steady and at an appropriate tempo, and encourages them to develop the ability to count silently in their heads. Suggest that pupils count *loudly* in their heads: counting must be physically felt, and the idea of 'loud'

◀ Chapter 6
Teaching Rhythm

counting in their heads has a very good pseudo-physical effect. If you do use numbers, it is helpful at slow speeds to count off-beats as 'and'.

**Combining pitch with rhythm**
When combining notes with rhythm, maintaining fluency (a steady pulse) is always the main objective. Before embarking on a piece of sight-reading, ensure that pupils know every note and understand all the rhythmic patterns. Fluency will not be possible if there is the slightest hesitancy in the recognition or understanding of either of these basic elements. Pupils becoming more aware of patterns in the music will further enhance fluency. In addition, it is essential that pupils learn to disregard errors – the psychological effect of making a mistake is often the cause of hesitancy. Once pupils learn to ignore mistakes they will be much more likely to play fluently and, with time, mistakes should eventually disappear entirely!

In addition, it is important to choose an appropriate tempo; maintaining a steady pulse will not be possible if they are suddenly faced with an unexpected and tricky technical passage. Preparing for such eventualities will be discussed below.

## Sight-reading as a multi-task activity

The act of sight-reading requires the co-ordination of an alarming number of simultaneous tasks. The basic elements (as already discussed above) are:
- reading notes and perceiving melodic patterns;
- understanding rhythmic patterns;
- combining rhythmic patterns with notes whilst maintaining a steady pulse.

There are also a number of associated factors:
- remembering the key signature;
- looking ahead;
- observing dynamic markings and other marks of expression and articulation;
- fingering (if appropriate);
- developing an aural understanding of the music;
- having some understanding of the harmony.

In fact, we 'multi-task' regularly. Watching television, eating a snack and carrying on a conversation simultaneously is not uncommon. The act of driving a car requires a combination of many complex 'driving' skills and the processing and interpretation of a variety of visual stimuli (other cars, pedestrians, signs, and so on) – and we may even be engaged in a conversation too! Multi-tasking itself is not the problem: it is learning to focus the concentration that is the greatest challenge.

Although it is difficult to teach concentration in the context of one reasonably short lesson a week, you can nevertheless continually draw pupils' attention to its necessity. Ask pupils, 'are you really concentrating?'. Tell them to clear their minds and concentrate fully on the matter in hand. Pupils will eventually learn to focus their concentration if repeatedly told to do so.

It is important to consider the above list of associated factors in more detail. Revisit each one regularly. Together they will result in efficient sight-reading. Of course, once a pupil is actually sight-reading, these points must become subconscious and automatic; concentration is focused simply on playing or singing the music.

### Remembering the key signature

Most young players don't think in keys. They tend simply to think in C major, adding the appropriate sharps or flats (if you're lucky!). It is important, therefore, to encourage pupils to *think in the key* by continually reminding them to do just that. Each time they play a piece in a particular key, talk about the key, ask them to play the scale and arpeggio and remind them to have the key in mind during the course of performing the piece. This will both heighten and maintain their awareness of key. You will need to reinforce this regularly until pupils begin to think in keys as a matter of course. The advantages are great. As well as being a much more musical way of reading music, such a discipline reduces the load on the short-term memory.

### Looking ahead

A typical music reader takes in a short pattern at a glance, 'processes' and memorizes it, and then plays or sings the music, at the same time looking ahead to the next pattern. This sequence is then repeated until the end of the piece. Pupils should be encouraged to read ahead – from the very earliest sight-reading they do. It is not necessary to prescribe how far ahead; by giving the instruction to 'read ahead' we are simply kick-starting the eye into its scanning mode.

Some teachers use a small piece of card just long and wide enough to cover up the music currently being sung or played, thus forcing the eyes to look ahead. There is something to be said for this; it will indeed cause the eyes to look ahead, but it also has the effect of restricting the regressive or backward glances that are very much part of the overall scanning process. So, although a good idea, the device should only be used on an occasional basis.

## Observing dynamic markings and other marks of expression and articulation

Whenever a note of music is played or sung it must, by definition, have a dynamic level; it is really a matter of laziness if the actual marked levels are not observed. Expression and articulation markings use simple signs (which should be understood) and language, which young learners are used to. It is up to you to insist that these markings are observed.

## Fingering

This problem is really restricted to keyboard and string players only. For wind and brass players there are very few notes that have alternative fingerings. Sometimes pianists will get into trouble because they run out of fingers; string players may find themselves in the wrong position. It is important to develop an instinctive approach to fingering; time spent playing scales, arpeggios and related patterns from a printed copy is a great help here.

## Developing an aural understanding of the music

The ability to see music and have some idea of what it sounds like is hugely valuable and is regrettably neglected by many teachers. In the act of reading words we do not need to speak them out loud to grasp their meaning – we know both what they sound like and what they mean internally. But the same is not so with music and this is a fundamental reason for lack of fluency and making mistakes.

The sequence of actions involved in music reading is usually:
    recognition of the symbol → physical response → *unexpected* sound.

A more musical and potentially successful sequence is:
    recognition of the symbol → a mental 'sound' → physical response → *expected* sound.

This sequence of events happens so fast as to be almost simultaneous.

Hearing music in your head is not a skill restricted to conductors, academics or other 'specialized' musicians. It can be learnt by anyone. The key is to be found in singing – from the earliest opportunities in a pupil's musical training. The first two notes a recorder player may learn might be B and A, but before they are played they should be sung, and before pupils are taught the symbols they should be played. Pupils should also be encouraged to hear the notes 'in their head' – even (and especially) at this early stage in their learning. The symbol on the page should not be first and foremost interpreted as a fingering resulting in an *unexpected* sound, but rather as a sound which is produced by a fingering, leading to an *expected* result.

Thus pupils should be taught to hear pieces through 'in their head' before playing. To introduce young pupils to this skill, ask them to sing short and simple phrases in their head first, then out loud, then play the phrase to see how close they were. Make this a regular part of reading music and accuracy *will* improve.

**Having some understanding of the harmony**

> Read the following quickly:
> He played really acccurately; and the musical shape and phasing was outstanding. He was never out of tune, in fact both the intonation and artculation was prefect.
> Now read it again. How many mistakes can you find?

Although there are spelling and grammar mistakes, the meaning is still clear. Similarly, if when pupils read music they have some idea of harmony, they will often be able to perceive the musical intention of a melody, phrase, chord or chord progression and thus, even at the expense of complete accuracy, present a musical rendition.

## How to teach sight-reading

Sight-reading can and should be taught. Some teachers advocate having a pile of music set aside for sight-reading purposes. This will work if the music is carefully chosen and appropriately graded; giving pupils music to sight-read which is too difficult for them is extremely damaging, especially at the earlier stages. Some teachers will play duets regularly – another good idea. In addition, there are a number of methods and graded sight-reading books available. Whichever method you favour, there are certain teaching strategies that should be common to all.

Rhythm is often the major problem when it comes to promoting fluency in sight-reading; so before any sight-reading exercise or piece is attempted, ensure the rhythm is understood. Before looking at the rhythm in detail pupils must take care to choose an appropriate tempo. They should learn to search for any pattern (be it melodic, rhythmic or technical) that may cause a slip if the tempo is too fast.

Once the tempo is decided upon, the rhythm should be tapped with one hand and the pulse with the other. Then reverse hands. Next, the rhythm is tapped with one hand and the pulse with the foot. Next reverse this! There are many permutations and you should try as many as you can think of. Rhythm is a matter of co-ordination, and the more exposure your pupils have, the better they will become. The next, and very important, step should be to ask your pupils to imagine the whole piece in their heads – as best they can. Reading the piece through in this way will provide a reasonably good idea of 'how the piece goes', and this will constitute a reference point – particularly important when pupils practise sight-reading at home on their own, with no one to correct their performance. You should also suggest they sing certain passages aloud.

When your pupils are playing the piece for the first time, remind them to look ahead (perhaps using your note-hiding device from time to time – see above). Insist on both absolute concentration for the duration of each exercise and that your pupils *count in their heads*; whether you ask them to count actual numbers or simply feel the pulse set up by their 'counting in' is really up to you. Finally, get the pupil to play the piece through, ignoring any mistakes.

After the piece has been played ask pupils to comment and criticize and then repeat the piece. The second playing should aim to correct any mistakes that occurred in the first play-through. This is a very crucial step in developing sight-reading ability. Revisit pieces after a few weeks and notice how much better pupils read them. During these sight-reading sessions talk about the various aspects of the reading process, described in the section 'Sight-reading as a multi-task activity' above, as and when you feel appropriate.

## Making mental plans
Good sight-readers will actually rehearse the next couple of notes a fraction of a moment before they play or sing them. Some modern psychologists call this 'making a mental plan' immediately before the action is carried out.

When preparing a sight-reading piece ask questions about the music. Draw your pupil's attention to important aspects and encourage them to become more aware of what they see. Asking questions will help the brain awaken to the idea of making these mental plans. By virtue of actually thinking and talking about notes and rhythms, melodic patterns, fingerings and expressive details, and indeed talking about the idea of making these mental plans, pupils will gradually build up a library of musical ideas and gestures that will occur time and time again.

### Skim-reading

Skim-reading music is a very good way of learning to assimilate a body of information in a short time. It is the way we often read newspapers or get the overall plan of a book. Try this 'game' with pupils:

> Ask them to run their eyes all over the music for 30 seconds, picking up as much information as possible. (This is the amount of time candidates should get at exams.) Now remove the music from their sight.
> - Can they remember the key or time signature?
> - Did they notice any scale or arpeggio patterns?
> - What was the first note?
> - Can they clap the opening few bars?
> - Can they sing the opening few bars?
> - Can they play any of the music from memory?
>
> When they become confident, try reducing the time for study to 20 seconds, then ten seconds; now make them take a 'snapshot' of the piece – two or three seconds only. Confidence will soon increase and they will learn to remember many details.

## Sight-reading in examinations

If pupils have been taught to sight-read methodically, then the 30 seconds or so that should always be given by the examiner should seem an ocean of time to the prepared candidate. What is the examiner looking for? Accurate notes and rhythms, observance of markings, musical and characterful playing, but perhaps, most important, a performance that maintains a steady pulse – even if it means a wrong note or two. Before sight-reading any piece make sure that pupils always have two of the most 'golden rules' of sight-reading at the *front* of their minds:

- **Always count** – or at the very least feel a steady pulse.
- **Never stop** – the importance of maintaining forward movement is fundamental.

# Chapter 8

# Teaching Scales

Scales and arpeggios are part of most exam syllabuses. They are perhaps the most difficult aspect of instrumental development to teach because young pupils tend to look upon them with anything from mild distaste to absolute loathing!

## Scales and technique

Scales are a fundamental part of technique – that area of musicianship embracing the control of all physical movement involved in playing an instrument or singing. Technique also controls tone, tone colour, intonation, dynamic level and rhythm. It is not merely a set of isolated physical or mechanical tasks, however; it is a means to an end – a means of inestimable importance. In performance, at any level, musicality will always be eclipsed if there is ever a struggle with the technical content. However musically well-intentioned the performer is, without technical control that subtle dynamic shading or rhythmic manipulation will simply not be possible.

Technique is, therefore, an 'umbrella' term comprising many areas of study; but in identifying all the component parts, it will be found that almost all of them can be dealt with by the study of scales and their related patterns. In addition to essential technical benefits there is another, almost more important, advantage to be derived from learning scales – the acquisition of a sense of key.

The prepared teacher will be ready to counter-attack the favourite moan of so many young players: '*Why* do I have to learn scales?'. It is important to spend time explaining and then constantly reminding your pupils of the reasons. They will eventually begin to see the huge benefits to be gained from regular and methodical scale study and, with some imaginative and relevant teaching strategies, they may even begin to enjoy their scale practice!

## Chapter 8

> Ask your pupil why *they* think scales are considered to be so important. Get them to write down their thoughts.
>
> Here are some reasons. Compare them with those your pupil has given.
> - Scales will vastly improve all aspects of technique, facility and control.
> - They will speed up the learning of new pieces because so much material is actually based on scale and arpeggio patterns – ask pupils to look at their latest piece and note down how many scale and arpeggio patterns they can find.
> - Learning to play arpeggios and related patterns will improve the ability to move around the instrument with facility and ease.
> - They will improve sight-reading ability because so many melodic patterns are based on scales and arpeggios.
> - Playing them well and with confidence will earn good marks in exams.
> - Finally, and perhaps most importantly, they will help pupils develop a sense of key.

## Teaching strategies

⬅ **Chapter 4 Motivation**

Having convinced your pupils that scales are indeed beneficial, the next hurdle is to find a way of including them in lessons and as part of a regular practice regime.

Methodical teaching is all important – the 'just get on and learn them' approach works for very few pupils. It is essential that you should never label scales as the least attractive part of an exam syllabus. Once said, it will be very difficult to change that perception – scales will forever be difficult both to teach and learn. In addition, they should never be left to the last minute in the hope that if a candidate can play a few there will be at least some marks to be gained!

Scale learning must be encouraged from the earliest possible stages; a methodical and progressive approach is necessary and there needs to be a sense of fun about the process. If the scale and arpeggio is seen as the final stage of an interesting and cumulative process, pupils will begin to lose their fear and distaste of scale practice.

### By ear or not by ear

In exams scales have to be played from memory. This often encourages learning scales 'by ear' as the principal (and sometimes only) method. Ideally, all pupils should learn and play scales both from the music and by ear. Recognizing the notated patterns is very helpful when learning pieces, and essential in building up a fluent sight-reading technique. Scales should never be learnt by simply feeling your way through; this will almost always result in mistakes and unrhythmic playing. Those players who get scales right the second or third time do not know them! Ultimately, a memorized scale is the result of many careful and thoughtful repetitions. Each separate action becomes the stimulus for the next – just as in the series of actions involved in, for example, tying shoelaces. The process becomes quite automatic after sufficient repetitions. Practising scales on a regular basis is therefore essential.

## Scale learning without scales!

Here is a strategy for approaching the learning of a new scale. It is a series of steps that will gradually build up confidence and lead to fluent and reliable scale playing. It relies on that tried and tested maxim: a house is as strong as its foundations.

> First of all pupils should write down the note names of the scale. (This is more important than you might think – to get the maximum benefit from scale practice, the mind must make a connection between the note name, the notational symbol and the physical action required to produce the note. You may find it a less than pleasant surprise to discover pupils do not actually know which notes they are playing. When attempting to teach music in a less compartmentalized way it is important that each of these connections is made.)
>
> Once the note names are known they should be said out loud both ascending and descending. Saying the names in descending order can be quite a task for some pupils!

**Chapter 11**
Simultaneous Learning

Many scales involve various technical problems. There are one or two useful publications that have identified these and that present series of exercises to be practised in advance of actually working at the scale. Alternatively, teachers who are prepared to devote a little time can devise their own exercises and perhaps photocopy them for their pupils' use. At first, this type of exercise should be practised slowly, with the music. Other elements of technical control (varying rhythms or dynamic levels for example) might then be added to extend further their scope and usefulness.

> Try some simple improvisation. Encourage pupils to improvise short tunes or pieces in the key of the scale being learnt. Keep reminding them to *think in the key*. These improvisations should include scale and arpeggio patterns as often as possible. They may even like to compose a short piece in the key – this may be little more than writing down their improvisation.
>
> Another useful 'game' to play that further develops key-sense involves choosing a famous tune and playing it by ear, in the key being learnt. It does not matter if it takes a few attempts to get it

**Chapter 10**
Improvising and Composing

> right; this is good aural training because the pupil is really listening and making appropriate corrections if necessary.

It is often worthwhile spending several weeks on preparatory work before pupils actually play a scale proper so that when they do finally come to playing a scale they have already built up a strong sense of the key and overcome specific technical problems. As you begin to teach scales in this rather more imaginative way, other teaching ideas will emerge and you will begin to be able to diagnose particular reasons for problems or weaknesses in scale playing. For example, a pupil who continually has real trouble playing a scale accurately may not be inwardly hearing the scale correctly. If a pupil is not confident in knowing what a scale *should* sound like, they are unlikely to know whether they have played it accurately or not.

> For those who find it difficult to hear a scale accurately in their head, try the following:
> - Slowly play the first five notes of a scale to your pupil a few times, asking them to listen carefully.
> - Ask the pupil to sing these notes, slowly, *in their head.*
> - Then ask the pupil to sing those notes out loud. Work at this until the intervals are correct and the singing is fairly well in tune.
> - Then ask the pupil to play those notes (by ear).
> - Once this is correct, work on the whole octave; again, persist until the singing is accurate.
> - As the scale is being played encourage the pupil to listen intently to the melodic shape.

By using this method over a period of time, you will instil a strong aural 'picture' of a scale, and thus build the necessary confidence. Use it to teach all the various scale and arpeggio patterns. Occasionally, play your pupil a scale including a wrong note. Ask them to identify the wrong note and whether the correct one should have been higher or lower. This is a useful method for spotting whether your pupil is hearing scales correctly.

For singers and players of variable pitch instruments (anything but keyboard instruments, in other words), introduce the idea of intonation and ask pupils to pre-hear each note before they sing it. Similarly, when playing the scale they should also pre-hear each note carefully first.

**Chapter 11 ➤ Simultaneous Learning**

Always have in mind the links between scales, aural and sight-reading and try to make these connections as often as possible.

At some point you will have to decide when pupils should be taught about the theoretical structure of scales. A method that combines theory with an aural approach would be ideal. For example, when teaching tones and semitones, always encourage pupils to inwardly hear, and then sing, these intervals. Simply knowing, for example, that on the piano a semitone is to be found by playing the adjacent key is not sufficient. This must be supported by an aural 'knowledge' of that interval.

## Making friends with scales

Encourage pupils to familiarize themselves with their scales, as they would get to know characteristics of friends or relations. Ask them to make a list of three or four features of each scale. Some of these may be obvious, others more particular. Here are two examples taken from actual lists made by young players:

Piano: F major hands together (Grade 2)
- Right-hand 4th finger on the B flat.
- Right-hand ends on 4.
- Thumbs together on F in the middle.

Clarinet: E major (Grade 5)
- It has four sharps – must remember the D sharp.
- Begins on right-hand E.
- The first three notes are all bell-note keys.
- Bell-note fingerings are the same in each register.
- It's my favourite scale (!).

Before asking a pupil to play a particular scale, always invite them to talk about it first; each scale will eventually acquire an identity of its own – pupils will really begin to know their scales.

## The perfect scale

Pupils should always aspire to play their scales as perfectly as possible. Here are the main characteristics of a really well-played scale:
- A scale should always be tonally even and played with some shape – the aim should be for a gentle arc with some sense of direction without the use of any excessive *crescendo* or *diminuendo*.
- Care should be given to maintaining control of tonal quality and dynamic level at the changes of direction.
- The first and last notes should be played without accents.
- Scales should always be rhythmically even, always demonstrating a secure and stable pulse, with care being taken not to lose rhythmic flow when changing direction.
- In *staccato* scales notes should always be played lightly and without accents, with all notes given equal duration.
- For non-fixed pitch instruments, scales must be played in tune.
- In exams all scales should be played at the same tempo.

## Practice strategies

You can set work based on the teaching strategies outlined above and with any luck pupils will actually begin to enjoy such an approach! Once the basic shape of a scale is 'known' there are an infinite number of ways to practise it.

It is really important that pupils listen critically to their scale playing. In this way they will begin to hear any inconsistencies of tone or rhythm, which is more than half the battle in developing the necessary control.

Here are some tried-and-tested strategies for scale practice:

- Practise using different rhythmic, dynamic and articulation patterns to develop technical fluency and rhythmic evenness. Scales need hardly ever be practised the same way more than once!
- Varying the tempo: slow practice for improving tone and intonation; fast practice for developing finger movement and fluency.
- Varying the accentuation (by playing in groups of 2, 3, 4, 6 or 8) will also develop evenness and control.
- For variety and a change of technical emphasis, begin at the top, descend and then finish at the top again.
- Begin scales on any note, such as B major beginning and ending on E. This is a very positive way to help develop key-sense and will sort out those who really know their scales from those who 'feel' their way through them.
- Play them *legato* ascending and *staccato* descending, then the other way around.
- Pianists can play one hand *legato*, the other *staccato*. Each hand can play a different dynamic level or shape.
- Where appropriate try different fingerings.

## Teaching modes

You may like to include the occasional teaching of modes in your pupils' scale studies. These scale-like patterns are the forerunner of conventional scales and are used extensively in jazz. In addition, if your pupil insists on playing D major with a C natural, even after constant exhortation, you can at least praise them for playing an accurate mixolydian mode!

# Teaching Aural Skills

## The point of aural training

For many, aural training conjures up memories of clapping back seemingly endless phrases, singing back awkward tunes or perhaps describing a short passage as modulating to the flattened submediant! Most 'aural tests' are concerned with pitch, rhythm or nomenclature (such as naming intervals, cadences and so on); this kind of work is incontestably necessary and important, but it is only part of the story.

Good aural training will cultivate a disciplined and musical ear, thus helping to develop the ability both to listen and to hear perceptively. Beyond scoring marks at grade exams, pupils will be able to play more musically, comment perceptively on performances, play or sing in tune, memorize music and sight-read more fluently.

This chapter deals with the broader issues of aural work rather than strategies for working at the particular tests in grade exams (though some thoughts in this area are discussed later).

## The musical ear

It is worth considering, if only briefly, what we mean by the expressions 'musical ear' and 'inner ear'. These, of course, refer not to our anatomical ear but rather to the part of our brain, or mind, that deals with thinking, feeling and responding to sounds. It is important to awaken your pupils to their musical ear; it is an essential tool in developing musicianship. The simplest way to access their musical ear is to ask them to sing a tune silently, in their heads.

The following activity will help your pupils discover the pathway from the inner ear to the physical expression of musical sound.

> Explain the sequence of events first:
> - A note will be played on the piano and your pupil is to listen to it intently as it dies away. (Alternatively, sing the note, or play it on your particular instrument.)
> - The pupil will then try to continue to hear the note internally for about 30 seconds.
> - The pupil should then begin to hum the note *pianissimo*, then gradually *crescendo* to a *forte*.
> - The note is then played again and the sequence repeated once or twice more.

## An ever-present ingredient

Aural training should be an ever-present feature of your teaching. There are an infinite number of ways that you can help heighten the aural perception of your pupils; it is through the constant asking of questions and the regular playing of 'aural games' that this will be achieved.

Consider the following:

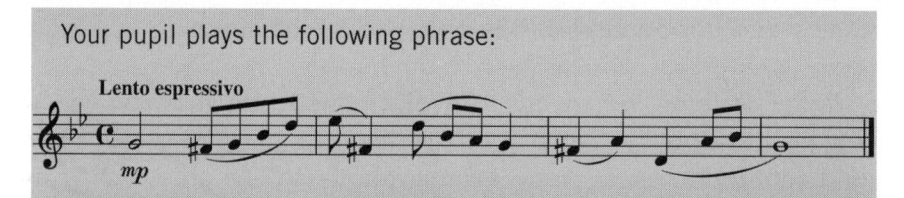

> Your pupil plays the following phrase:
>
> [musical notation: Lento espressivo, mp]
>
> If, for example, they played the final note of this lyrical phrase unmusically, with an accent, you might ask them: 'Did you play the end of that phrase effectively? What is the character of the phrase? Did the end relate well to that character?'
>
> Now you play the phrase to the pupil three or four times, each time varying the dynamic shape and weight of the final few notes. Ask for each of your phrase endings to be imitated by your pupil. Which one was preferred? Why? Can they think of any other ways to end the phrase?

Instead of simply telling your pupil how you would shape that phrase – which they still may or may not be able to do – let them think for themselves. They will have been made to think about the music, to listen, to copy and, finally, to make their own informed and musical decision. This is an example of practical aural training which, with imagination, you can adapt for virtually any teaching situation.

> You might continue the lesson, using just the final four notes of the phrase:
> - Ask the pupil to name the interval formed by the first two of these notes.

> - Can your pupil play a fifth beginning on a completely different note?
> - Now sing a few fifths.
> - Ask your pupil to play that four-note cadential figure in a succession of different keys.
> - Next, without the music, play the four notes, but in a different order. Ask your pupil to hear them in his or her head first, then play them back.
> - Repeat, changing the order again. Use your third order as the start of a short improvisation.

This sort of aural work can continue as long as your imagination will allow – and once you begin working in such a way you will find it leads you in all sorts of fascinating directions.

**Chapter 11 ➤**
Simultaneous Learning

## Using the voice

Singing is an essential activity for all musicians. Encourage all your pupils to sing in a choir if at all possible. The act of singing will enhance their perception of pitch, phrasing and intonation; it will help them to develop their 'inner ear' and to improve sight-reading. Encourage them to *support* their sound.

It is now fairly universally considered that no one is completely 'tone-deaf'. There are strategies for helping the 'one-noters'! Here are two:

> - Ask your reluctant singer to sing a note; you must then quickly find it on the piano. Play the note back for your pupil to sing again and

> repeat a few times until it becomes reliable. (Often you will hear them sing you a different note after you play them back their original note.) Gradually move to a new note, perhaps a semitone or tone up or down from the original. With much praise, patience and cajoling you will begin to hear improvements.
> - Ask your pupil to sing their highest note, and then their lowest. Play further games similar to the above but with a range of notes and do not worry about absolute accuracy for a while!

Once pupils are able to sing reasonably confidently, use the voice often in lessons. Ask them to sing phrases – in their heads first and then out loud. Ask them to sing scales and arpeggios, trying to hear the next note *before* they sing it. Ask them to sing through their pieces. Can they sing them from memory? For some, these tasks may seem immensely challenging, but the confidence they will build is invaluable, and the improvement in both a pupil's musicianship and ability to master grade exam aural tests will be marked. It is certainly worth the trouble!

## Playing and singing in tune

The development of reliable intonation is essential for all musicians. Pupils who wish to progress to an advanced standard will need to learn to hear intervals accurately. A well-tuned piano, electronic tuning device or, at the very least, two or three tuning forks, will be necessary. Intonation practice should be undertaken regularly and you should continually draw your pupils' attention to poor intonation. Pianists should be encouraged, if at all possible, to play only on pianos that are in tune.

From time to time concentrate on a single interval. First hear the interval in the head. Sing it, then play it. When playing scales pupils should learn to hear and sing each note *before* it is played. Play or sing scales, passages from pieces, or just single notes in unison with your pupil; ask your pupil to comment on the intonation. You can usefully adapt this kind of work for group-lesson teaching.

## Memory

Traditional aural tests in grade, diploma and university exams rely heavily on short-term memory skills. There has recently been a gradual move toward introducing more perception-based aural tests and this is to be applauded. However, memory still plays an important part in aural skills and these will need to be approached methodically and progressively. Performance from memory will be dealt with in Chapter 15.

Recent research has divided memory into three 'layers'. The first layer, the pre-short-term memory, lasts for perhaps less than a second. Nevertheless, it is long enough for perception and understanding to take place. If a phrase such as 'the cat sat on the mat' or a picture of one's mother was flashed on a screen for less than a second, understanding would probably take place because both images are stored and 'known' in the long-term memory. Information that is fed into the short-term memory (which may last for several seconds) will only be fully processed and comprehended if the information can be related to 'known concepts' or knowledge in the long-term memory. As soon as new input is understood (i.e. connected to something already known) that information will go into the long-term memory.

## Aural and memory

Improving aural skill requires a certain degree of understanding of the complex workings of the memory. A brief investigation into the major/minor dilemma should begin to stimulate a more considered approach to the processes involved in aural training.

How can a pupil 'know' that a piece is major or minor? Is it simply because major sounds happy and minor sounds sad? These particular polarizations may be considered rather contrived (though some would argue it is all in the harmonics!) and are arrived at principally by association. Recognizing major/minor is really dependent on matching what is heard with what is already 'known', in other words with what is stored in the memory as major/minor. Thus, the more pupils listen to music, the more opportunities they will have to build up a memory of major/minor, and the more efficient they will become in determining which is which. They will, in effect, be developing *auditory memory*.

While auditory memory is central to the development of certain aural skills, it is not the only factor in solving the major/minor issue. Pupils should additionally be taught about the intervals making up the two different triads, thus providing information to be stored in the 'intellectual' memory. The more internal connections being made (i.e. the more ways they know something), the greater the understanding and the quicker and easier it will be to recall them. Nonetheless, teaching major=happy, minor=sad is another very useful connection to make and will probably always be part of major/minor identification.

## Specific aural tests

We shall consider a number of strategies for each of the common forms of aural test and, where appropriate, try to identify how to access the relevant memory skills.

### Clapping or tapping back a rhythmic phrase

It is important that you begin by establishing a steady and reliable pulse. Particular rhythms that are to be tapped back should be ones that have already been studied in some way so that a connection with those in the long-term memory store can be made. These connections will be virtually instinctive, but to make them work it is important that practice be regular.

At whatever grade level you are working, always start with short and simple phrases, gradually increasing length and complexity. Repeat phrases as many times as necessary to allow your pupil to get them right.

Discuss the rhythms, and perhaps even suggest that your pupil writes them down. Aural skill is dependent on knowing as well as simply responding. The link between hearing a pattern and knowing its notation will also strengthen the connection with sight-reading.

### Singing back a melody

Begin with very simple melodic shapes. Make up shapes that pupils will 'know', such as those based on scale patterns. Only very gradually add to the length and complexity. Pupils should always be made to feel comfortable and confident when singing, and you may have to spend a lot of time in achieving this end! Praise them whenever possible.

There are two ways pupils can practise the singing back of phrases:
- Responding immediately (required for the present ABRSM response tests).
- Hearing the phrase in their heads first before singing.

Work at both methods with pupils. Suggest that they play back melodies on their instruments occasionally and then try to repeat the shape in other keys. Identify the names of particular intervals from time to time. Rather than simply going through as many examples as possible in a short session, spend time on one or two examples only and work at them until they can be sung accurately, with each interval heard and understood. This will have a much more useful and long-term effect on developing this skill.

### Identifying intervals, cadences, chords, major/minor etc.

The correct identification of these musical concepts is concerned partly with auditory and partly with 'intellectual' memory. It is essential to practise this skill repeatedly over an appropriate length of time in order to reinforce the internal auditory memory. This will accelerate the process of recognition (of a particular cadence for example) and recall (identifying it as a perfect cadence based on those heard previously). Also discuss the theoretical aspects of intervals and cadences, and ensure that pupils are aware of them as they appear in pieces being learned. Take them out of the context of the aural test and allow pupils to perceive them as part of their daily musical thinking.

### Perceptive listening

Pupils should be encouraged to listen to music intelligently and often. Recommend that your pupils attend (school) concerts; you may even occasionally like to organize a group visit to a public concert. Encourage them to listen to music on the television and radio. Even listening to signature tunes (rather than simply hearing them) is worthwhile. Perhaps you might ask pupils to write a few lines describing what they heard. Here is an example from a nine-year-old after listening to a popular signature tune on the television:

> It starts off with a piano playing the main tune. The piano is mainly *staccato*. It has a steady drum beat in the background. It has little sequences on an electric guitar. It gets a lot more softer near the end and a lot slower.

The listening section of the ABRSM aural tests requires some knowledge of technical terms, style and period; some discussion of these topics should be a regular part of the learning of pieces.

## Spotting mistakes

There is presently a test in the ABRSM syllabus that asks the candidate to perceive a change made to a rhythmic pattern. The broader implication here is the development of critical listening. In practising this test you might like to ask your pupil to repeat the first version before you play the altered version. In order to develop the benefits of this test even further, encourage pupils to identify changes with greater accuracy and detail than may be expected at an exam.

Play through pieces to pupils, adding your own changes for them to identify (both with and without the printed music in front of them). These may be anything from altered notes, rhythms, dynamics, faulty intonation, to stylistically inappropriate playing and so on.

# Chapter 10
# Improvising and Composing

Creative ability is essential for all musicians. It is, in essence, the ability to make informed and artistic choices. Though performer and composer may be considered to inhabit different worlds – for the performer the choices concern dynamics, phrasing and tempo, whilst for the composer they concern notes, rhythms and timbres – both can, and should, learn from one another. For young performers, therefore, improvisation and composition can be very useful and valuable ingredients in the development of their creative imaginations.

## What is improvisation?

Many people will think of jazz when the word 'improvisation' is mentioned, but improvisation need not have anything at all to do with jazz. Improvisation is, in a general sense, creating music as it is being performed. This can indeed range from the most complex and sophisticated jazz to the invention of a simple and repetitive rhythmic pattern, or a series of some (seemingly random) low notes 'representing', for example, an elephant.

It is also a technique that is required in particular musical genres. In addition to the improvisations of jazz, the realization of figured bass-lines and ornaments in Baroque music, and the creation of cadenzas in classical concertos, are both forms of improvisation. Organists will be required to improvise (or extemporize – a word interchangeable with improvisation) at strategic points in services, and modern composers occasionally call for improvisation in their music. Improvisation is central to much music-making in the Middle East, Asia and South East Asia. All these forms of improvisation have been dealt with comprehensively in numerous excellent books and, whenever appropriate, should be taught as part of a full instrumental training. In this chapter we shall consider ways of using improvisation more generally as part of instrumental and singing development.

## Why improvise?

There are a number of reasons why a young player might spend part of a lesson or practice session improvising:
- improving aural skills;
- improve technical skills;
- increase general musical awareness;
- develop confidence;
- explore the instrument;
- explore music without notation;
- cultivate self-expression;
- develop skills required in certain exams;
- develop a facility in a particular musical genre;
- develop the inner ear and the ability to think ahead musically.

## Practical uses of improvisation and working without notation

### As part of aural training

Because improvising demands the ability to hear sounds, process them and, almost instantaneously, decide what to do next, it can be a powerful tool in aural training.

Begin with rhythmic 'question and answer' work:

> Tap out a simple two-bar phrase that is then 'answered' by your pupil. This can easily be extended into a musical 'conversation', and the length and complexity of phrases increased progressively.

Once pupils become confident with rhythm, introduce melody:

> Start with simple three-note patterns, gradually increasing the number of notes used and the complexity of the melodic shapes. Again, as confidence grows, develop this idea into an extended 'conversation'. As you work at these 'improvisations', gradually introduce the concepts of repetition and variation, balance and resolution.

### Improvising exercises to improve technique

Certain technical problems may have to be overcome by a lot of repetitive practice. By putting a particular interval or melodic pattern into various rhythmic contexts, for example, practice becomes more interesting and creative. It also transforms potentially monotonous, passive repetition into an active process of imaginative thinking. This can be taken a stage further by encouraging pupils to improvise tunes that include the technical problem.

### Increasing general musical awareness
Improvising in keys is a wonderful way further to strengthen key sense. Pupils should play the scale and arpeggio first and always keep the key in mind as they are improvising. As pupils progress you can introduce the concept of modulation.

◀ **Chapter 8**
Teaching Scales

Pupils can develop their awareness of intervals by choosing one and improvising a whole piece around that one interval. One week's practice could be based on seconds for example, with the pupil bringing you a 'prepared improvisation', complete with appropriate title!

Pieces can be improvised on particular dynamic levels, tempos, forms of *staccato* and accentuation and so on. Pupils will get to know and understand these musical concepts much more vividly by thinking and working through them in this way, rather than by simply being told what they mean.

### Developing confidence
Pupils can be encouraged to improvise to, or indeed with, family or friends. On the most basic practical level, this will simply result in yet more time spent playing or singing. On a more sophisticated level, it may inspire many hours of creative musical fun and thus help to strengthen confidence and musicianship. Pupils can open up pathways into their own musicality through improvisation, and this may well add a sense of spontaneity and clarity to their performances of notated music.

### Exploring the instrument
Learning by notation is necessarily a somewhat slow and restrictive process. Young players are keen to play lots of notes and explore the sounds their instruments are capable of making. There is no harm done by encouraging pupils to improvise short pieces using a wider palette of notes and rhythms than those already known through notation. Depending on the particular instrument, you may feel it prudent to offer some advice and recommend certain guidelines as to how far pupils can go without dampening their enthusiasm!

### Self-expression through improvisation
Encourage pupils to improvise musical sound-pictures depicting scenes, activities or people. This will effectively engage their imagination in a simple and direct creative process. If they would prefer a less focused activity, many will find pleasure in simply 'expressing' themselves by a kind of musical 'doodling'.

### The development of skills required in certain exams
There are certain tests in musicianship (and other) exams that require improvisatory skills. These may be to improvise on a particular melodic or rhythmic pattern, an interval or chord, a poem or picture or perhaps over a given harmonic sequence. Practice of whichever form is favoured

by the particular pupil is essential, but pupils should be able to improvise in response to any given stimulus.

## The development of a particular musical genre

Thus far, all the uses of improvisation discussed focus essentially on generic musical skills rather than genre specific ones. On the other hand, learning to improvise in the jazz idiom, to realize a figured bass or to extemporize a fugue requires considerable skill, assimilated through many hours of teaching and practice. It is not within the scope of this book to offer particular advice on these highly specialized techniques; there are many excellent methods available. However, these skills are within the reach of many, and the experiences gained by including them in lessons on a regular basis will be invaluable.

## From improvising to composing

There has been a lot of unnecessary polemic and ink spilt determining at what point an improvisation becomes a composition. By refining, imposing one or two rules and perhaps notating it in some way, we transform an improvisation into a composition.

As soon as pupils have begun the process of learning to play or sing they should be encouraged to improvise/compose their own little pieces. Even after the very first lesson suggest to pupils that they make up their own tune using the notes and rhythms so far learnt and perhaps attempt to notate them in some form using staff or graphic notation. Through this practical involvement with the materials of music they will come to understand and learn more quickly. Some guidance from you will help, but once under way many pupils will immerse themselves enthusiastically in this kind of work.

> The first piano lesson might introduce 'middle C' (in both right and left hand), via a tune that uses $\frac{4}{4}$ time, crotchets/quarter notes and minims/half notes and the four-bar phrase. Using these materials, suggest your pupil make up a further (similar) tune. Find out whether they have a pet or interest that can serve as the inspiration and title.

Through this encouragement of simple composition you are:
- teaching them some theory through creativity;
- teaching them how to notate music;
- monitoring, through getting them to handle the materials, whether they understand the concepts;
- encouraging them to spend just that little bit more time on additional musical pursuits at this crucial period of learning.

## Chapter 11

# Simultaneous Learning

## The problem

Try this investigation and make a note of your findings.

> During a 'typical' day's teaching, note how much of each lesson is spent working on pieces (and studies) and how much on 'other' aspects (aural, scales, sight-reading and 'musicianship'). Be accurate (and honest!).

You will almost certainly discover that the greater proportion of your time is spent on the teaching and learning of pieces. The reasons are obvious and understandable – 'tunes' are really what most young players want to spend their time learning and, in our (generally) grade exam-orientated climate, it is the pieces that gain the most marks and therefore require the most attention and preparation. Furthermore, rather than setting the agenda for each lesson, teachers find themselves simply reacting to whatever pupils have (or, too often, have not) prepared. Teaching is often no more than correcting mistakes. As a result, progress is slow, teachers get bored and many fundamental areas of musical development are marginalized. Furthermore, we are not instilling in our pupils the very important means to 'do it themselves'.

It is through the teaching of sight-reading, aural skills, scales and related patterns (and other technical work) that we can develop a young musician's 'technique' (in its widest sense), musicianship and, ultimately, self-reliance. Many teachers would reluctantly admit having to relegate scales and sight-reading to the last five or ten minutes of a lesson (if at all) and then often to lose even those precious few minutes to preparing some last-minute aural work in the final few lessons before an exam.

Clearly this is not ideal.

## The solution

The need is to find a method of introducing sight-reading, aural work, scales, and other means of developing musicianship on a regular basis and to make their presence interesting, relevant and stimulating. Given the little time available, an integrated approach would seem to be the answer: integrating aural work with pieces, scales with sight-reading, aural work with scales and so on. The ingredients of musicianship can be both taught and learnt much more effectively when they are seen as being part of a whole. The objective is to make each lesson much more like an organic process. The teacher sets the agenda, is pro-active rather than re-active, and there is a considerable amount of pupil–teacher interaction throughout. This is what is meant by *simultaneous learning*.

Just as each and every pupil is an individual, so the method and content you adopt will be both flexible and varied. What will work for one may not work for another; your emphasis and proportional use of 'ingredients' will be slightly different from pupil to pupil. The following ideas are presented as food for thought; they are intended to represent a list of these ingredients for you to combine and experiment with in your own personal way. One of the great advantages of this style of teaching is that you can never be sure in what direction a lesson might develop – a lesson becomes a voyage of discovery rather than yet another trudge over very familiar territory.

The asking of questions and transference of much of the thinking and problem solving on to the pupil is central to this kind of teaching. Some pupils will find having constantly to answer questions both stimulating and easy to handle; others will be more tongue-tied. Encourage them and wait patiently for their answers; try not to hurry them. Gradually their confidence *will* grow.

## The simultaneous learning lesson

Two lesson scenarios are given below. The first combines simultaneous learning with more conventional teaching; the second is a more 'advanced' simultaneous learning lesson and is entirely based on developing musicianship skills.

### Lesson scenario 1 – piano

Your pupil has been practising the C major scale and the first section of an *Allegretto* (carefully chosen for being in C major) by Czerny Op. 599 No. 36, from *More Romantic Pieces for Piano*, Book One (ABRSM).

The focus of this lesson will be to:
- further develop a sense of C major;
- improve the playing of the C major scale;

- use the music learnt as a starting point for aural, improvisation and other musicianship work;
- improve the first section of the piece.

> Begin by asking your pupil to play a scale of C major. Ask them about C major:
> - Does it have a colour?
> - Does it have any distinguishing features?
>
> Ask your pupil to say the notes of the scale, up and down. Then the scale should be played in each hand separately. Ask questions:
> - Was the sound even?
> - Was the fingering well controlled?
> - Was the rhythm even?
>
> The scale should be played again a number of times, each time with a different focus (chosen by either pupil or teacher), such as varied dynamics, different rhythms or groupings, and various combinations of dynamics and rhythms.
>
> Choose a well-known tune and ask for it to be played by ear in C major. Now improvise a short piece in C, either for right or left hand – decide on a shape beforehand (e.g. ABA). Discuss it, and play it again.
>
> Remembering a phrase from the improvisation, use it to initiate a series of aural 'games'. First you play a series of two-bar phrases and your pupil repeats them. Then, instead of repeating the phrase, your pupil responds with an answering phrase.
>
> Turning now to the piece, begin by looking at the left-hand part. Play the first eight bars and then discuss the harmonic shape. Try the left-hand part from memory. Discuss the dynamic shape and its relation to the changing harmony.
>
> Try to improvise a simple right-hand part over the actual left-hand notes. Try this from memory.
>
> Learn to sing the right-hand melody. Try singing the melody whilst playing the left-hand part.
>
> Ask the pupil to play just the right-hand first bar. Ask them to try playing this melody beginning on other notes. Ask them to perform the first section. Discuss the qualities of the performance:
> - Was it in time?
> - Did the phrases have shape?
> - Did the dynamic shape enhance the melodic line?
> - Were there any technical difficulties? If so, what strategies could be used to help?

> Now look at the left-hand part of the second section. Discuss the harmony; *think* through the hand positions.
>
> Ask the pupil to sight-read the music. Were there any errors? Ask them to play the music again, focusing on removing any mistakes.
>
> Finally, set work for the next lesson:
> - Improvise or compose a short Allegretto in C;
> - Do more work on the C major scale;
> - Begin work on the C major arpeggio;
> - Learn the second half of the *Allegretto*.

### Lesson scenario 2 – any instrument

The focus of this lesson is to develop musicianship skills.

This lesson will involve a little pre-lesson preparation. You will need to choose a piece of sight-reading, but take a little trouble over this: the key (and scale and arpeggio) should be familiar. It may be the particular key of a piece, song or study your pupil is learning. Your chosen sight-reading piece should be technically well within the capabilities of your pupil.

> Begin by asking your pupils to identify the key of your chosen piece, then put the piece to one side.
>
> Ask them to play or sing the scale and arpeggio of that key, after having first made sure they understand the key signature and that they know the notes. This might be followed by some technical work on, for example, weakness of tone, unevenness of rhythm or some tricky fingerings; encourage your pupils to *listen intently* to their performance so that, with your guidance, they can suggest any necessary remedial work. The importance of getting your pupils to 'take ownership' of their playing is essential; do this by encouraging continual self-criticism.
>
> Now try some imitation exercises. Using the same key, sing or play a short, simple melodic phrase that you then ask your pupil to sing back or play back on their instrument. As well as reproducing pitch and rhythm (the mainstays of most exam aural tests), ask them to imitate, to the best of their ability, your tone, dynamic levels, intonation (where appropriate) and any other musical 'shaping' or phrasing. Keep your phrases very straightforward to begin with – playing back is more difficult than singing back, but you should find, as time goes by, that this exercise really will improve your pupil's aural perception.
>
> If you're teaching an instrument rather than the voice, ask them, sometimes, to sing the phrases back (similar to the ABRSM aural test in the early grades); you might sing the phrases yourself – there

are many permutations. You can use more 'grade-based' aural exercises at this point if you wish, but always try to make them practical and related to the key-of-the-day.

At this point you might slip in some improvisation. Still in the same key, use as the opening idea one of your imitation phrases, or a phrase from the sight-reading piece. Decide with the pupil beforehand on the musical parameters – aimless doodling (whilst certainly having its place) is perhaps not appropriate here. Decide how the pupil might 'use' and even develop the material, some kind of overall structure (AB or ABA for example) and how long the improvisation is to be.

After the pupil has played their improvisation, discuss the success (or otherwise) of the performance:
- What was the time signature?
- How was the material used?
- Which dynamic levels were employed?
- Was the structure clear?

and so on.

Perhaps, if there is time, repeat the improvisation, but now with adjustments and improvements.

Finally, we come to the sight-reading piece. There are many ways to bring this into the integrated learning process; you might begin by asking your pupil to glance at the opening two bars – or at least the opening phrase, for a few seconds. Remove the music from sight and ask the pupil:
- What was the time signature?
- Can they clap the rhythm?
- Can they sing the melodic line?
- What was the tempo mark and dynamic level?
- Were there any other expression markings?
- Can they play any of it?

Now allow a further glance through, with the purpose of spotting repeated shapes and scale and arpeggio patterns. Again, cover the music and ask the appropriate questions. If time permits you can continue this process, looking at modulations, technical or rhythmical difficulties, structure, musical shape and climax and so on. In this way, and in a relatively short time, we are stimulating and developing that all-important *musical awareness.*

Now ask for a performance and then, again removing the copy, discuss it:
- Was it accurate?
- Were there errors?

> - Was it a musical performance?
> - Were all the expression markings observed?
>
> Ask the pupil to play the piece again. If you have time you might ask them to try playing it again from memory.

As you move through this simultaneous learning process, remember to build up confidence with repeated encouragement and praise. If the ideas do not seem to work for a particular pupil do not give up! You may have to rearrange the ingredients or try new ones. As you begin to develop your own approach you will discover an infinite number of ways of connecting and cross-referring from one discipline to another. It is a method of teaching that grows organically and feeds off the imagination (of both teacher *and* pupil!).

## Making connections

Simultaneous learning can be used from the very earliest stages of teaching. In those crucial first lessons most teachers rely on a three-stage process. First, pupils observe a *notational symbol*, then we describe the appropriate *physical action*, and finally the *sound* is produced. Unfortunately, most teachers (and thus pupils) tend to think of these elements as though the one leads on to the next (and in the particular order just stated). In fact, they should always be simultaneously cross-connecting.

By teaching:

> notational symbol → physical action → sound

pupils will often become dependent on notation and, almost certainly, will not know what the music sounds like until it has been played. The strong internal impulse will be for notation (first and foremost) to cause a physical reaction (a fingering or whatever) rather than a sound.

As your confidence grows in teaching simultaneous learning, begin to think of different ways of connecting these elements; perhaps most important is that musical notation should lead straight to knowing how the music will sound without having to make the physical action first:

> notational symbol → sound → physical action

Singing is at the heart of this technique, and young pupils should therefore be encouraged to sing before playing on a regular basis. It is also worth considering other kinds of musical activities, such as composition and improvisation, that result from further altering the order to, for example:

> sound → physical action → notation

## Simultaneous learning for the beginner pupil

The simultaneous learning style can be used to great effect with beginners. Once you begin thinking along these lines you will discover an endless variety of strategies you can employ.

> A beginner wind player might have been taught to recognize three different notes and the semibreve/whole note note-value in their first lesson. In their second lesson you might ask them to sing four-beat notes (semibreves) whilst clapping the pulse. Then ask them to play their three notes for four beats each (no music at this stage). Discuss the quality of the sound:
> - Was it even?
> - Was the counting accurate?
>
> Now ask for the notes to be played in a different order. If you are working in a group the other players can then repeat the new order.
>
> Now arrange your pupil(s) so that they are not looking at you. Using just these notes, play them a series of three-note patterns (varying the order each time and including repeated notes). Your pupil(s), either individually or as a group, then repeat them. Now get your pupil(s) to write down (compose) their own three-note pattern. Before they play the pattern ask them to sing it.
>
> Now you can move on to playing through work they may have prepared and to introducing new material, always remembering to sing melodies and clap rhythmic patterns before they are played. Make sure that you are continually asking your pupils questions to confirm that there are no gaps in their knowledge or misunderstandings in their grasp of new material.

This lesson will have combined work on technique, notation and reading, aural, rhythm, improvisation and composition. It should easily fill a typical-length first lesson – in fact there is probably enough here for two lessons – and you will find that once you begin using this more flexible approach your lessons will develop in all sorts of interesting and possibly unexpected directions.

## The sliding scale

Consider a sliding scale of teaching styles: at one end is the most rigorous kind of 'conservatoire-model' teaching, in which the broader picture tends to take second place to detailed study. At the other end of the scale is the most 'organic' style of simultaneous learning. Each pupil will require teaching at a different point on the scale; but by adopting this flexibility and discovering what gets the best out of each pupil you will find teaching becomes much more fulfilling.

Taking on this method requires a certain degree of courage. It takes time – time you might otherwise have spent correcting wrong notes in pieces or reminding your pupil that there was a *crescendo* here or there. But the great advantage is that once you have begun to build, strengthen and stimulate your pupil's actual 'musical ability' you won't have to make such comments so often. Your pupils will have begun to develop the ability to learn for themselves, to notice more, to increase their musical awareness. This approach to teaching is probably only a short step from what many imaginative teachers do anyway, but having embraced it you should perceive a noticeable improvement in your pupils' practice; they will begin to be more self-reliant and that means you have more time to teach them *music*.

# Chapter 12

# Group Teaching

There is perhaps no other subject that arouses as much passion amongst instrumental teachers as the mention of the words 'group teaching'. The immediate responses are often as varied as:
- I love it. My beginner string groups are the highlight of my working week!
- It's impossible. How can you possibly have players of differing abilities playing the same piece?
- Real teaching can only be done one to one. There's no other way.

## Some background as to why we teach instruments individually

Much of our teaching today is modelled on ideas developed in the late 18th century. These were refined during the early part of the 19th century through the 'conservatoire' model (in other words the one-to-one, master/apprentice approach); the same model that now underpins most of the work in our conservatories. In the United Kingdom, the growth of instrumental teaching, from the mid-20th century onwards, was dominated by the pervasive influence of this one-to-one teaching style. Now, at the beginning of the 21st century, there is a growing awareness of the positive benefits that may be derived from a group teaching and learning situation.

One-to-one conservatoire teaching usually relied principally on a well-motivated pupil rather than a particularly effective teacher. This style of individual teaching, essential for the piano, was also adopted by other instrumental teachers. The outcome is that a small number of learners achieved high standards of performance whilst a much larger number of potential learners either gave up the struggle soon after beginning tuition, or were denied the opportunity to learn in the first place, having failed the selection process.

## The development of group teaching

The emergence of instrumental group teaching in schools happened perhaps rather more by accident than design. In the United Kingdom Local authorities found themselves with generous amounts of Government money (with which they could buy instruments) and a lot of enthusiastic pupils – but not enough teachers. Though the money *was* generous it was insufficient to pay for the much larger body of teachers that became necessary in order to cater for so much potential one-to-one teaching. Thus, teaching in groups offered itself as a solution by default to a difficult problem. As a consequence, methods for group teaching developed through the imagination and experimentation of good and committed teachers, rather than through carefully devised and co-ordinated teaching plans.

A great deal has been written about group teaching for class teachers, based on action research in classrooms, but instrumental and singing teachers are less fortunate: very little work has been done on this important topic. The work of Professor Kevin Thompson in the 1980s is important. He explains that:

> Individual and group-taught students received more or less the same spread of time to the various aspects of learning in music, with the exception of notational skills. In spite of group-taught students having received less time in this category, their level of achievement in fluency of notation was disproportionately high. Perhaps teachers made fewer repetitive statements in group settings and saved instructional time. This, coupled with the possibility of learning from others, may account for the alacrity with which the group-taught students acquired notational skills.

Kevin Thompson observed four colleagues working both with individual pupils and with groups of up to eight pupils. Interestingly, he found that the balance of activities within the lessons was about the same in both situations.

## Preparing for group teaching

If you are intending to teach in groups, it must be with the clear knowledge that you need to give a good deal of thought to how you will deal with this very different kind of teaching situation. Group teaching will only be successful if the pupils are reasonably well matched in age, standard and learning ability. If possible, you should be able to move pupils from one group to another in order to allow them to mix with those closest to their own abilities and learning speeds. Groups might be reviewed at the end of each term to determine whether each pupil is in the one most appropriate to their current standard.

Ample time must be allowed for preparation, and this will almost certainly need to be significantly greater than in one-to-one teaching. The selection of appropriate material is very important and potential problems and various ways of overcoming them should be thought out beforehand. Perhaps most important is to ensure that all group members are occupied for the full duration of the lesson. A 're-active' teacher could get away without any lesson preparation for one-to-one teaching, but in the group situation any kind of disorganization, lack of structure or momentum may have a very disruptive effect.

Your teaching room should be spacious and you should work out how it is to be set up and where pupils will sit or stand. You should clarify your ground rules for behaviour at the first lesson and always expect these to be maintained.

## Strategies for group teaching

Once the lesson is under way, it is essential to keep all pupils involved and occupied. Ask questions, and continually switch pupils from playing to active listening. Here are a number of activities you can try:

- Those not playing can either clap the melody others are playing or play the rhythm on a percussion instrument.
- Make appropriate arrangements of pieces you intend to use, with certain parts consisting of simple long notes.
- Have the whole group play warm-ups, pieces and studies together – an excellent intonation test.

> - Spend some lessons developing group improvisations.
> - Encourage the more able to compose for the group (you may have to help quite a lot here, but the results will be well worth it).
> - Pupils should be encouraged to comment and criticize (positively). Get them to notice faults in others; it will have a very beneficial effect on their own playing.
> - Play duets, trios, quartets or other ensemble music.
> - Have group concerts from time to time.
> - Try to have some percussion instruments available in your teaching room. Pupils can be encouraged to improvise simple rhythmic accompaniments to pieces being learnt. For example, those not yet able to play the tune might be given an accompanying part.
> - Play to your pupils, asking afterwards for comments on how you played certain phrases, your use of dynamic levels (and so on).

## Simultaneous learning in group teaching and the meaning of progress

The principles of simultaneous learning are, of course, ideal for bringing to the group teaching lesson. It is important, however, to accept that the traditional kind of sequential learning might not always be appropriate. The kind of progression whereby one week you teach the note G and crotchets, and the next week you teach F and quavers (and so on), will often not work as well in group teaching. You will have to adopt a much more imaginative and lateral approach. Once you get into the habit of teaching in this way, you will find endless strategies to use and you will find your lessons developing in all sorts of fascinating directions. Your pupils will make a lot of progress, but perhaps not in the same way as in one-to-one work.

Perhaps this is a good time to consider what you understand by *progress*. Because our society is so dependent on the measurement of 'progress' by success in exams, other forms of progress may not be acknowledged. This is unfortunate since progress may also be more broadly perceived in terms of developing musicianship. Consider for a moment whether there are any aspects of musical development which are not obviously examinable or which don't necessarily develop in a 'straight line'.

Here is a possible lesson scenario for using simultaneous learning in your group work:

> You have a group of four flute players; they have been learning for about six months and have all been specifically asked to prepare one octave of the G major scale for the lesson, and a piece from their tutor book. The main object of the lesson is to become more

> familiar with the key of G major and to improve some basic areas of technique.
>
> Begin the lesson with all playing G in unison. Discuss the intonation. Revisit important aspects of breathing technique.
>
> Then player 1 plays G for four beats 'passing' the note to player 2, who passes it to player 3 and so on. Discuss the tone quality. Were all players playing their notes evenly? Was each G in tune? Was the quality of each note the best each player can manage? How can the quality be improved?
>
> Now discuss G major. What is the key signature? Are there any fingering difficulties to be aware of? Ask one player to play it. Others then comment on the performance. Was it in time and in tune? Was the fingering precise? Was it rhythmical, and so on? Then get the whole group to play the scale. Then try it at different tempi, different dynamics, articulations etc.
>
> Then ask one player to make up a short tune (or phrase) in G major (no longer than, say, two bars). Discuss the phrase. Then, using this phrase, improvise a piece, each player taking it in turns to play (player 1 begins, then player 2 takes over without a break, then player 3, player 4, back to player 1 and so on). You might even join in too. What is the mood of the piece? Perhaps you might have time to try it again.
>
> Have a very easy piece of sight-reading ready (in G major). Ask the players to look at the music and try to hear it in their heads. Ask them to sing it. Then ask them to play it.
>
> Now play through the piece they have prepared during the week. Play as a group first, then individually (if there is time); ask the other players to make any appropriate comments on the performance.

The overriding principle governing this, and similar, simultaneous learning lessons, is that all the pupils are *actively* involved all the time, whether playing, listening or commenting intelligently and musically. That is the essence of successful group teaching.

## The occasional group lesson

If you don't regularly teach in a group, organizing a group lesson, perhaps once a term, may be a very useful occasion. Give the group lesson a theme. Scales, studies, the preparation of a particular piece or overcoming anxiety would all, for example, make good topics. Your pupils may be a little tongue-tied or self-conscious to begin with, but with some gentle cajoling they will relax and enjoy the experience of

← Chapter 2
Age and Approach

playing to each other and sharing ideas. Perhaps the occasion might end (or begin) with some refreshments, thus allowing your pupils to get to know each other better socially.

## Practical considerations

There is no doubt that teaching in groups means more preparation and planning, and it is likely that the teacher will spend much time writing arrangements. For this reason alone, many may regard it as non-viable, given the daily pressures on their time. There is little doubt, however, that the gains, both economic and educational, from group teaching are substantial. For example, the private teacher working at home could teach four pupils in 45 minutes, instead of just one, and the hard-pressed school could double or treble its number of instrumental pupils by providing group lessons (even though some instrument sharing may be necessary).

## Chapter 13

# Teaching Pupils with Special Requirements

### Being musically gifted

It is most likely to be a parent who first detects certain unusual characteristics in their young child. Between the ages of about three (sometimes earlier) and five or six, the child may ask repeatedly to play a musical instrument. They will sing often, and in tune, enjoy dancing or moving to music and will often ask to listen to music, which they will do with focus and attention. Such a child may be musically gifted. Once in the care of an experienced teacher and with the appropriate backup and support this child may very quickly develop into a highly talented musician. But prodigious musical gifts are not solely in the possession of the very young. Many great and established international performers and composers have had to wait until their teenage years (or even later) for their talents fully to emerge.

**Further Reading and References**

There have been a number of very detailed studies made recently about the development of the young child who demonstrates extraordinary musical ability. The actual mental processes involved are not really within the scope of this book (interested readers should refer to **Further Reading and References**) but it is important to know something about the mind of the gifted child. A parent may ask you whether a child is indeed gifted, or you may begin to see characteristics emerging in your own pupils. At some point you will need to decide whether you wish to teach that child, or whether you feel it appropriate to recommend a specific teacher with particular experience working with the highly talented. In addition, you may find yourself having to advise on whether the child should go to a 'normal' school, with many musical activities taking place elsewhere, or whether they should consider some form of specialist music education.

## Identifying the characteristics

There are some general characteristics and conditions that seem to be peculiar to all highly gifted children (whatever their speciality). These will, of course, be found in different proportions from one child to another, but you should be able to identify all of them to some degree:

- The child will show evidence of a vivid imagination and creative sense.
- They may demonstrate an above-average intellectual capacity (though this need not be outstandingly high).
- They often have the ability to focus on one task for a considerable time and there may be a degree of obsessive behaviour.
- They may show high levels of motivation, determination, self-discipline and commitment.
- They may display great reserves of energy.

You will also notice in the gifted young musician some, or all, of the following specific characteristics, which will be markedly more refined and advanced than in more normal children of a similar age:

**Pitch** They will be able to sing melodies in tune, perhaps have 'perfect pitch', be able to remember melodic phrases and to identify notes played harmonically.

**Rhythm** They will be able to maintain an even pulse, have a quick response to subdivision in different tempos, and be able to repeat rhythms accurately.

**Psychomotor skill** They will demonstrate keen muscular co-ordination and develop digital agility quickly.

**Timbral sensitivity** They will show concern for the quality of sound.

**Musical imagination** They will show sensitivity to melodic shape and tonal colour.

## The problem and the solution

Having identified the child as being musically gifted there will be a host of decisions to make:
- What kind of provision will have to be made at home?
- What kind of school would be most appropriate?
- Who should take on the responsibility of actually teaching the child?

If you are known to the parent or are indeed teaching the child, you may well find yourself involved in solving these problems.

Broadly speaking, music will have to become a central focus of daily life. For parents, many hours will have to be devoted to transportation (to lessons and other musical events for example), and a good deal of money will have to be found for paying for all of this (as well as for a very good instrument).

Whether the child goes to a specialist music school or a more 'normal' school will depend on the personality, commitment and determination of both child and parent. Specialist education has its pros and cons: the necessarily single-minded nature of such institutions may be too restricting for some, while others, who have stayed the course, might find entering the real world somewhat dispiriting. On the other hand, for the gifted musician who may be considered 'odd' in the context of a normal school, the musical, sympathetic and thus understanding environment of the specialist school may constitute the only way to survive. There is no doubt that specialist schools do nurture exceptional talent in a caring and focused environment, but it is important that those considering these schools are highly self-motivated.

It goes without saying that a lot of thought should take place before making the decision.

## Teaching the highly gifted

Teaching the highly talented requires much more than just technical and musical guidance. You may find yourself playing the part of teacher, counsellor and possibly even 'life-manager'. The demands made on a teacher by highly gifted pupils are considerable. To meet these demands it is essential that you have a very discerning ear and a vast array of imaginative and challenging strategies for all circumstances. In addition, it is desirable that you have a deep and analytical understanding of technique, a good knowledge of 'performance' repertoire and an understanding of the stresses related to performance. You will need great reserves of energy and long concentration spans – gifted children have both in considerable quantities!

If you can see yourself in this description, teaching the highly gifted may well be possible. If you feel a little doubtful, then be confident in passing the pupil on to someone who has the appropriate experience, remembering that it in no way demeans a teacher to do so. It is salutary to consider that the teacher who deals with the highly talented would probably be lost in the very specialized world of teaching beginners, or the type of cumulative and progressive teaching necessary in developing the more typical young player.

There is a further, complex and indeed profound problem that teachers of the highly gifted must somehow come to terms with. Your pupil may soon develop a technique far beyond your own; they may shape a phrase in a way that had never occurred to you; they may develop extraordinary musicianship skills. You will have to find a way to deal with this. There is no simple answer – it will be found only by a lot of soul searching. When teaching the highly gifted it is important that you find some way of presenting an air of confidence to your pupils and avoid ever becoming intimidated by the situation. Finally, be honest; never bluff – you will always be found out!

## The ageing prodigy

Progress for the pre-adolescent prodigy will be generally unhampered by psychological obstacles. Young children, whether gifted or not, love mastering increasingly complex tasks and may hurl themselves without inhibition into their musical studies. The onset of adolescence, however, brings with it uncertainty, instability and a new set of impulses. Perhaps the major problem for the gifted young musician is to reconcile the desire for freedom from the family while at the same time maintaining a continued devotion *to* the family. The shrewd teacher (and parent) will prepare carefully for this time by allowing the growing musician the 'personal space' and independence required.

For the exceptional prodigy, and perhaps those who win high-profile competitions, careers may begin much earlier than for the more normal person. By the age of 20 they may have performed extensively and achieved something of celebrity status. It is important to look at those few who have achieved this kind of success – there has been much written about them – and learn both from the high and low points. Some have gone on to become distinguished figures in the musical world; others have found their lives moving in confusing and unhappy directions. Careful consideration should be given to just how the career might develop; slight changes of direction may be necessary to avoid loss of interest, boredom or disillusionment. Prodigies (and their parents) should never be afraid to seek counselling, or, at the very least, maintain open lines of discussion with teachers and other professional careers advisors. An instrumentalist may also be advised to cultivate an interest in conducting or teaching, for example. The learning of languages may also be of great consequence as an international career unfolds.

## Pupils with special educational needs

In general, people today will probably interpret the expression 'special needs' as meaning some form of learning difficulty (dyslexia for example). Music, however, will also attract children with physical limitations, children who have visual impairment or a hearing loss, children with severe learning difficulties and those with behavioural or emotional problems. To help and guide this minority of children there are highly trained music therapists and other specialists, and you should know where to steer parents if they come to you for advice.

### Dyslexia

Sometimes pupils who appear to display symptoms of what might be described as laziness, or who seem uncharacteristically slow to grasp apparently simple concepts, or who have particularly poor short-term memories, may in fact be dyslexic. The word 'dyslexia' comes from the Greek meaning 'poor language', but gone are the days when dyslexia simply implied problems with spelling or reading. Much exciting scientific research has been, and is being, carried out, and as a result considerably more is now understood about the condition, although there is still a long way to go. What has become clear is that the dyslexic brain works differently from the non-dyslexic brain. Connections engendered by both visual and auditory stimuli are not necessarily made in the logical way that would be expected of the non-dyslexic brain. Poor short-term memory difficulties often give rise to secondary problems, such as lack of concentration, disorganization, frustration, erratic behaviour, anxiety and, in particular, lack of self-esteem.

The other side of the coin is that dyslexic pupils are often extremely imaginative and creative, and display an enviable degree of innate musicality. Although many teaching methods will be similar for both dyslexics and non-dyslexics, it would be inadvisable to make any assumptions and you would be wise to rethink your teaching methods – possibly radically – in terms of each dyslexic pupil. Often it is the music teacher who may be the first to recognize dyslexia in a pupil; alternatively it may be brought to your knowledge by a parent or the school. Sheila Oglethorpe's excellent book *Instrumental Music for Dyslexics* is full of eminently practical advice and clear strategies and should be read if you do find yourself involved in teaching dyslexic pupils.

**Further Reading and References**

### Dyspraxia

If you notice a pupil who continually has problems with eye–hand co-ordination, or who has difficulty understanding and processing sequential skills (even, for example, putting an instrument together), they may be *dyspraxic*. Dyspraxia often coexists with dyslexia in the same person; it is a condition that affects the control of movement. Recent research has suggested that a significant number of people may well be affected – perhaps as many as ten per cent of the population.

There are many signs that a pupil may be dyspraxic:
- They may look messy.
- Their response time may be slower than normal.
- They may have very short concentration spans.
- There may be confusion over laterality, with pupils getting frustrated over right and left.
- They may show symptoms of clumsiness; they may display difficulty in judging heights and distances and they may keep forgetting and losing things.
- They may also show signs of emotional problems, perhaps getting quickly depressed, frustrated or anxious.

If you feel a pupil does indeed seem to display the above symptoms then it would be appropriate to speak to a parent or the member of staff in an institution who deals with such problems. They may refer the child to a doctor, educational psychologist, occupational therapist or similarly qualified person. There are, however, many strategies that you can undertake to make learning easier for those who may be dyspraxic.

Try teaching in such a way that the pupil has very few things to think about at any one moment. Break down each new skill, concept or new piece of information into the smallest units possible and patiently reinforce verbal instructions many times. Allow more time than normal for the completion of a task, or for the pupil to fully grasp any new concepts or skills. Encourage the pupil to make lots of use of organizational tools. For example, emphasize the importance of the notebook, using it to spell out very clearly indeed *exactly* what and how the pupil should practise. And, finally, give the child as much encouragement and praise as possible.

Section Two

# Beyond the Lesson

# Practice

It is impossible to overestimate the vital importance of practice for the developing musician. Regrettably, though, for many young musicians, practice is perceived as monotonous, arduous work, often done under duress when they would much rather be playing with friends or watching television. In fact, if we are honest, quite a number of young musicians do very little practice indeed. So what is to be done? It is certainly the teacher's responsibility to present practice as a positive, rewarding, enjoyable and fulfilling experience – but *how* do we do this?

## What is practice?

The central purpose of practice is to progress – to solve problems, to develop and broaden musicality, to *think* about the music. Practice is the time when your pupils, with your guidance, take on the responsibility for their own improvement and development. Reflect for a moment on your own attitudes towards practice and on how you present practice to your pupils. Ask yourself the following questions:

- Do you enjoy practising?
- What makes you practise?
- Do you teach your pupils *how* to practise?
- Do your pupils practise effectively?
- How do you evaluate effective practice?

## The principles of good practice

Pick up any book on learning or playing an instrument and you'll probably find a section on practising. Although some offer the same fundamental advice, many prescribe vastly different approaches. Herein lies an important message: there are many successful strategies for practice. The universal feature, though, is that efficient and productive practice generally demands a continually *active*, *creative* and *thoughtful* approach.

# Chapter 14

Let us examine practice from two extreme viewpoints. At one end of the scale we have what Keith Swanwick calls *encounter-based* music education, in which improvement occurs not by practice, but by virtue of belonging to an amateur orchestra, choral society or brass band (for example), attending rehearsals (regularly) and 'playing-through' (practising) the part occasionally at home. Development, as a result, is clearly going to be something of a hit-or-miss affair. For some, this may constitute all the 'practice' they do. At the other extreme we find the highly efficient teacher, prescribing a carefully thought-out, progressive and sequential daily routine involving all aspects of musical and technical work, with indications of how often and how much time should be spent on each. Where you pitch your own expectations between these two extremes will depend on a number of factors:

- the potential shown by the pupil;
- the degree of enthusiasm they exhibit;
- the importance the pupil attaches to music;
- the extent of parental support (or indeed support from other relatives or friends);
- the lengths to which you, the teacher, are prepared to go to ensure your pupil lives up to your expectations.

Certainly, you should expect regular practice. No significant improvement will be made without it. It's best, however, to be realistic and perhaps not lay down hard-and-fast rules that will inevitably be broken. Psychologists tell us that human beings enjoy a certain degree of routine in their lives. Suggest, therefore, that practice takes place four or five times a week, perhaps at a regular time: before or after breakfast, before supper, before or after a favourite television programme. With luck it should become an important and enjoyable part of the day – especially as your pupil will begin to notice real improvement as the days and weeks go by.

Occasionally, your pupil may be too tired or not in the mood. There is little point in practising under such circumstances and, if this is a reasonably rare occurrence, pupils should not be made to feel guilty. Mental and physical alertness are both essential. Always stress that it is the *quality* of practice that counts – not the *quantity*. If practice is perceived by your pupils to be a positive, enjoyable and constructive affair, they will eventually become willing to spend the necessary time to overcome the challenges you set them. 'Challenge' is the key word – some children rise to a challenge, while others tend to shy away from it, perhaps from fear of failure (see under 'Practice and anxiety', p. 100). You need to adjust the way in which you present practice to suit the temperament of the individual child. In time, your pupils may begin to generate their own internal motivation – the ultimate goal in teaching pupils about practice.

## What makes people practise?

There are a number of reasons why some pupils practise and some don't. For those who don't there are ways and means that can be employed to help; in any case, most pupils will need some cajoling and a certain amount of gentle persuasion. The art is to know your pupil and then decide which method, or combination of methods, will achieve the most positive results. Here are a number of ideas to consider:

**The 'carrot' approach** Perhaps the most reliable method is to set short-term goals – an exam, a performance at a school or private concert, a festival or a competition.

**Setting specific tasks** Be *very* specific – for example 'learn D major descending and the first line of a study from memory'.

**Form filling** Some young people *like* filling in forms, so give them a daily practice chart which includes exactly what they should practise and for how long, and plenty of boxes for them to tick.

**The pupil-centred method** Ask your pupil what *they* would like to practise and what they think they *ought* to practise (and why).

**Practice as internal challenge** Just as sport enthusiasts will have the necessary internal drive and motivation to 'train' hard, sometimes young musicians will exhibit similar characteristics. If you can perceive this in any of your pupils, harness it and encourage it – it is a powerful motivational force.

**Pleasing the teacher** Some pupils will want to practise well to please the teacher. Praise and encourage often and you may find this to be the case, but bear in mind that ultimately pupils must learn to practise for themselves; too much dependence on a teacher could become a problem.

**The enjoyment factor** Occasionally you may find a pupil really loves a particular piece and will spend hours practising it. Always be on the lookout to find such pieces because the 'knock-on' effect can be very strong.

**Parents** Some parents get very involved with their children's musical development and will always encourage (and sometimes reward) practice. This can be very helpful, as long as they reinforce what you are trying to teach! For parents who *are* keen to help their children (and as long as the child is happy to accept parental involvement) you could diplomatically suggest how best you feel they can play their part:
- by reminding the pupil to practise in the first place and by making space (temporal and physical) for them to do so;

← Chapter 3
Lessons

- by helping the pupil to practise *effectively* (see below);
- perhaps simply by requesting a performance of pieces or even some scales currently being studied.

**Bribery** Even some quite eminent teachers have resorted to this (usually rather successful!) method. To be used with discretion!

## What is good practising?

Young musicians need to be taught how to practise well. In a sense, the whole lesson may be perceived as a preparation for the practice sessions that take place between lessons. After all, each week your pupils should practise (with careful encouragement) for anything up to five or six times longer than the lesson.

### The beginner

Good practice habits must be inculcated from the very start. Consider the first few lessons: your new pupil will be learning very short pieces, so practice will inevitably be very repetitive. (This is not something to worry about – young beginners quite enjoy a lot of repetition!) It is necessary, though, to make interesting and imaginative suggestions that will avoid 'practice as repetition' becoming mechanical and the only association your pupil makes with the concept of practice.

> Teach your pupils to:
> - listen;
> - play with different dynamic patterns;
> - learn from memory;
> - play with their eyes closed;
> - improvise or compose other pieces using the same notes.
>
> Make sure that your new pupils know exactly what they are to practise and exactly how to practise it.

### The developing player

As your pupil begins to develop, continually mention the importance of slow practice and of listening with a critical ear to everything they play. Mentioning an idea once is not enough – you must repeat it again and again. Continually remind pupils to take care over details, for this is the means towards quality performing.

Teach them how to identify and focus attention on particular areas and work at them in a methodical manner. Working on difficult sections should always be a primary focus, and pupils should know how to break down pieces and sections into small manageable units.

As you introduce new rhythmical patterns or new techniques, make sure pupils understand them and then discuss how they can be practised. Begin to *ask*, rather than tell your pupils how they might practise a new technique.

Gradually increase the number of different tasks they are to perform in each practice session, but always clearly explain their purpose.

Never ask a pupil to practise something they don't fully understand or see the reason for. As above, the same two fundamental rules always apply: the pupil should know exactly *what* to do and *how* to do it. Always enquire how practice went. Were there any problems? What went well? Bring practice to the foreground of learning.

### More advanced players

By now your pupils' practice should be both efficient and effective, and they should be able to perceive when they are practising well. At this level it should be all absorbing and the highest level of concentration should be maintained. They should also now recognize the fact that really good practice *is* hard work and will not always bring about instant (or even short-term) improvement. As technique and musicianship continue to improve, it becomes increasingly difficult to make obvious progress. But with sustained and diligent work progress will be made, and playing or singing will become more and more confident and reliable.

# Practice strategies

## The practice room
The temperature should be comfortable, the room well ventilated and as free as possible from distractions (perhaps a large and colourful 'Do Not Disturb' sign could be hung on the door to deter unwanted visitors and suggest that mobile phones are switched off!). If such a situation is not available at home, then maybe arrangements could be made for the pupil to practise at school or perhaps at a friend's house.

## Pupil's demeanour
Suggest that your pupils practise in a relaxed, unhurried and methodical manner. A serious level of concentration is required if the session is to be of real value. Remember that most people (of whatever age) find it very difficult to maintain intense concentration for long periods – so it is important to suggest that pupils take frequent (short!) breaks during their practice.

## Practice content
A basic formula for successful practice is to see each session as a 'reconstruction' of the lesson. Warming-up exercises, technical work, pieces, sight-reading and perhaps playing through old pieces will all be part of the weekly practice requirements. Be very clear what you expect to be practised, and suggest and discuss a variety of practice methods and approaches. List them in the notebook and be sure to hear what you asked for in the next lesson. Always remember to praise good work.

## The practice notebook
Practice benefits enormously from thorough planning, especially in the earlier years. The notebook is essential here. Set out each week's practice details carefully and don't forget to explain what each instruction means. Keep the notebook neat, and encourage pupils to make notes too – such as particular technical or musical problems they find especially difficult and with which they need more help. Perhaps they might note down the title of a piece they heard played at a school concert or by a friend that they would like to learn.

## The teacher's practice diary
Efficient teachers will always keep an accurate record of the lesson and what is to be practised. (A blank Lesson Plan/Record Sheet is provided at the back of the book.) Pupils who know this are less likely to assume they can get away without practising the appropriate work, and 'losing their notebook' will no longer be available as an excuse!

→ Lesson Plan/Record Sheet

## Critical listening
It has often been said that the key role of the teacher is to be a 'pair of ears'. Teaching your pupils to listen and hear critically is possibly the greatest skill you can give them. Never miss an opportunity during

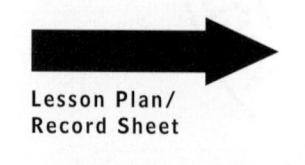

← Chapter 9 Teaching Aural Skills

lessons to draw their attention to anything that might develop this skill.

> Use the following (or other similar) questions when appropriate:
> - Was that a good sound?
> - Was it appropriate to the music?
> - Were the dynamic levels well related?
> - Was that *crescendo* effective?
> - Was that note in tune?
>
> and so on.

These are the questions that should constantly be going through their minds when practising. In a sense, during practice, your pupils should be in continual conversation with themselves.

## Practice by repetition

A lot of practice will inevitably be repetitious. For this kind of work to be really beneficial it is essential to have a reason every time a section, phrase or pattern is repeated. If there is an obvious technical problem to work at pupils should get into the habit of asking themselves:

- What and where is the problem?
- What causes the problem?
- How can the problem be put right?
- Would there be any point in varying the repetitions?
- How might this be done?

When the whole process is active and thoughtful, practice will be very effective.

## 'Mechanical' practice

Mechanical practice, practice with the brain disengaged, indeed any kind of thought*less* practice is, on the whole, to be discouraged. However, occasionally you may need to prescribe exercises simply to overcome a muscular weakness or develop some particular finger independence – in this case 'mindless' repetition might be acceptable!

## Practising pieces

When approaching a new piece, make sure pupils know at least something about the composer, when the piece was written, the meaning of the title, the character and mood of the music, and understand any Italian markings. (It is surprising how little pupils often know of these points but what a difference it makes when they have done some research.)

A lot of slow playing should take place, encouraging pupils to listen critically to themselves, correcting their mistakes as they go along, just as the teacher would at a lesson. You will, of course, have your own favourite methods for overcoming technical and musical problems, but here are a number of well-tried ideas.

> Suggest to your pupils that they:
> - practise a short section at a time;
> - repeat short sections – but always make sure they know why they're repeating them;
> - practise using dotted rhythms for tricky passages;
> - break up fast passages into small units;
> - learn sections from memory;
> - transpose sections into different keys from memory (which tests how well you *really* know a passage);
> - try passages out on a different instrument (if the pupil plays one) or sing them.

Using the above ideas (or others of your own), make sure you have discussed appropriate practice methods in relation to the particular piece or section of a piece to be practised. Pupils will eventually learn to make such decisions for themselves. Further ideas for practising sight-reading and scales are given in the relevant chapters.

⬅ **Chapter 7/8**
Teaching Sight-Reading/
Teaching Scales

**Practising practice**

A useful technique in the teaching of practice is either to demonstrate a few minutes of effective practice, or to ask pupils to practise in front of you (for anything up to say ten minutes if you like). Make notes that will then provide a basis for detailed discussion afterwards. This also works well in the context of group teaching.

## Pupils who do no practice

Some pupils, either through lack of time, facilities or inclination, even with your best efforts, putting many of the above strategies into play, will still simply not practise. Because so little progress will be made, most of these non-practisers will probably give up playing after a while. There will, nevertheless, be some pupils who *can* make progress and who do derive pleasure simply from attending and playing in lessons. The power of the brain is such that it can process and develop even when no practice takes place. So, whilst some pupils would be better spending their time in other pursuits, others may indeed benefit from such an approach. It is for the teacher to be sensitive to the situation and decide on the best course of action.

## Practice and anxiety

Lack of practice may be the result of a deeper sense of anxiety. There are various defence strategies young people adopt and it is well to look out for these if you notice a reduction in enthusiasm and progress. In addition to poor, or indeed no, practice (which will usually be supported by endless 'valid' excuses), pupils may 'forget' to bring their music to lessons, may engage the teacher in constant 'red-herrings', will often avoid eye-contact or may be entirely uncommunicative.

Often the cause of these symptoms is the fear of failure, and pupils will reckon that it may be better not to try at all than to try and fail. If you suspect this to be a likely reason behind a pupil's negative responses it will be necessary to talk through the problem with great care and sensitivity. Perhaps the music or technical demands being made are simply too difficult and the pupil feels intimidated to the point of near or absolute inertia. A dramatic change of direction will be necessary, together with a great amount of encouragement. In time the situation may right itself. Don't feel you have continually to challenge pupils – sometimes (quite lengthy) periods of consolidation may prove invaluable in building confidence and thus making practice both enjoyable and productive.

## Does practice make perfect?

Without entering into a lengthy debate on the philosophical meaning of perfection, the answer is, broadly speaking, yes it does. However much practice we do, few will attain a state of absolute perfection, but for the majority, practice will certainly make for progress, particularly if certain criteria are met:

**Appropriate resources**
- Pupils must be prepared to devote time, in both quantity and quality.
- Practice facilities should be pleasant and inviting.

**Motivation**
- Enthusiasm must be maintained.
- Parental support and encouragement must be maintained.
- Successful practice should be rewarded.

**Effort**
- Pupils must be prepared to work hard.
- Practice must always be effective.

The last point is very important. If a pupil is not maintaining a high level of care and concentration, allowing mistakes to go uncorrected, playing incorrect rhythms (and so on), then practice will make anything but perfect. The pupil is simply practising to become a worse player! Rather than 'practice makes perfect', perhaps a more realistic aphorism would be, 'careful practice makes for progress'.

It might be helpful to conduct a review of your pupils' progress in terms of the effectiveness of their practice:

> Make 'case studies' of a number of pupils, outlining ways you think they can improve their practice. Discuss your thoughts with the pupil concerned, in the context of asking *them* how they think they can practise more effectively.

## A practice checklist

You will find many lists, in tutors and methods, of important points to remember while practising; here are those that are fundamental whatever your instrument. Try to encourage your pupils to adhere to them closely.

- Check for a good posture – the way you stand or sit and (if applicable) the way you hold your instrument – using a mirror, if possible.
- Always aim for a beautiful tone quality.
- Listen to your tuning.
- Listen carefully and critically to *everything* you play.
- If you make a mistake, correct it immediately. Don't simply go back to the beginning for another 'run up'.
- Check that you are observing all the markings on the music (dynamics, articulation, phrasing, etc.).
- Is the rhythm correct? Use a metronome from time to time.
- Practise playing slowly rather than quickly.
- Are you thinking about the character of the music and ways of communicating your musical ideas to your audience?
- Occasionally 'perform' during practice – no stopping, come what may.
- Always try to imagine what your teacher would say – and act on it!
- Occasionally try studying the music away from your instrument – hear it 'in your head', think about fingerings, analyze the structure and so on.

# Chapter 15

# Preparation and Performance

As young players progress there will be ever more opportunities for performing. There are the didactic occasions – exams, festivals and competitions – 'formal' performances, school concerts, recitals that form part of school exams at secondary level, and so on. There are also a whole host of informal opportunities, among them playing with friends and family, playing at religious services and community events, and taking part in musicals or amateur operatics.

## Preparing music for performance

Pieces chosen for performance, whatever the occasion, must be prepared thoroughly. Technically, nothing must be left to chance and interpretation should be deeply considered. Playing with style and the ability to interpret music do not come naturally to the vast majority; these are skills that need to be taught. However, through the process of teaching, players should ultimately develop the confidence to interpret for themselves.

### Teaching 'style'

Unless pupils come from a musical family, are musically well informed, go to concerts or listen to music intelligently, responsively and often, they are unlikely to have an innate understanding of musical style. Performances, at any level, will rarely be musically convincing if they lack stylistic awareness. A sense and understanding of style has, therefore, to be taught.

Style is the result of consistently applying certain characteristics and qualities to a performance, and will necessitate a certain amount of knowledge and research. These qualities will emerge as a result of knowing something of the composer, the historical period in which the music was composed, performance conventions of that period and geographic and nationalistic influences. Thus, for example, in preparing a performance of a Courante by J. S. Bach you will have to take the following into account:

- aspects of the dance itself;
- the characteristics of the French Courante (as opposed to the Italian Corrente);
- appropriate ornamentation;
- the characteristics and performance possibilities of the instrument the work would have been written for, such as articulation, tempo and the appropriate range of dynamics to be used.

**Further Reading and References**

For the really determined pupil you might even research the characteristics of Bach's own keyboard and study such books as Stephen Hefling's *Rhythmic Alteration in 17th- and 18th-Century Music*.

In this way your pupil will be able to build up a stylistic performance. Encouraging pupils to listen intelligently to recordings by eminent players is, of course, very beneficial. But as players advance they should not become restricted by concerns of style. The great pianist Schnabel warned his pupils (who were, of course, *very* advanced) against stylistic generalizations. Although style needed to be understood, each work had to be considered on its own merits.

## Teaching interpretation

Interpretation is the act of turning notation into sound. It is the synthesis of stylistic awareness and musical imagination, resulting in an effective re-creation of a particular composer's music. But there is much more to it than that. In the act of interpretation a developing musician must be taught to consider *all* aspects of the music in relation to the style, character and expressive intentions. Decisions have to be made, and these are principally concerned with tempo, phrasing, rhythm, dynamic levels and other markings. During the study of a piece of music you should discuss all these features with pupils, passing on historical knowledge and performance convention where appropriate. Ultimately, you will hope to transfer a good deal of the decision-making to your well-informed pupils. Here are a few points of discussion under each of these main headings:

**Tempo** The clues to finding an appropriate tempo will be in the composer's words (usually in Italian), sometimes a metronome indication, the time signature and the character of the music. All these features will depend, to a certain extent, on historical convention, and so the dedicated teacher will either do some homework or guide pupils to appropriate textbooks where this information can be discovered.

**Phrasing** This is the grouping of notes into musically meaningful units. Articulation, accentuation, dynamic levels, tone colour and rhythm will all need to be carefully considered in the shaping of notes into phrases. If you are not a singer, consider the music as though it were being sung.

**Rhythm** Decisions concerning where to place accents, and the precise duration of notes, will have to be made. Note-values have much more to do with the character and style of the music than the fact that, for example, a minim/half note lasts for two beats.

**Dynamic levels** The range of dynamic levels marked by a composer represents a point of departure and is, of course, 'relative' rather than 'absolute'. Subtleties of phrase shape will result from the use of many dynamic gradings and colours well beyond what any composer might mark in a score. It has been said that the composer gives you about five per cent, the rest is for you to decide. Perhaps this is something of an exaggeration, but it certainly gives an idea of the possible scale of your input!

**Ornamentation** In a sense, this is very much a matter of informed choice. You should feel confident to alter or re-write the realization of ornaments (even in exam material!) if you consider there to be a more effective, more imaginative, or simply an equally appropriate, but different solution.

**Other markings** An understanding of all relevant markings – articulation, accentuation, and all written terms – should be part of the learning process. The meaning of these will often depend on the historical period of the music, and an informed performance will show evidence of this knowledge.

You should be careful that having finally arrived at an 'interpretation' it is not a rigid one, in which everything feels worked out to the last detail. Teachers should always encourage a certain degree of spontaneity in performance – a little *rubato* or shading of tonal colour, for example, may transform a competent and well-prepared performance into an inspired one.

## The performance

Performing is a different type of experience compared with practising and playing through pieces in lessons. It is the moment when the thoroughness of the preparation will really pay off.

Pupils must be taught that a performance begins immediately they enter the room or hall (or exam room) and does not end until they leave it. Physical movement should be poised and dignified, never abrupt or nervous. The audience should be acknowledged with a smile or a bow if it is a formal concert. Tuning up (if appropriate) should take as long as necessary. During the performance the mind should be focused on the music, or on practical matters such as making eye contact with other players, as necessary, and if there are any distractions, internal or external, advise your pupils to refocus their mind as quickly as possible. You can practise dealing with external distractions by, for example, deliberately distracting a pupil during a trial run-through – open a window loudly or drop some music. Discuss how easy it was for your pupil to ignore these distractions – or whether it took them a moment or two to re-focus.

At the end of a performance they should remain absolutely still for a few moments before relaxing. Audience applause should be acknowledged with a smile and a bow – nothing too extravagant. Just a small bow of the head will do if your pupil is self-conscious. If the performance is an important occasion you should help your pupil overcome any anxiety over correct bowing. The stage or room should be left with care.

## Performance anxiety

Anxiety and nerves cannot be eliminated absolutely. All musicians experience nerves to a varying degree and, to a certain extent, they are beneficial in both engaging the concentration and creating the right conditions for an exciting and vivid performance.

> Ask your pupils:
> - To what extent they feel that nerves affect their performances?
> - In what physical ways these nerves manifest themselves?
> - In what mental ways nerves affect them?
> - Do they feel that being nervous has a positive or negative effect?
> - Can pupils identify particular causes of anxiety?

Physically, nerves may affect your pupils by causing a fast heartbeat, sweaty hands, shaking, dry mouth, tension, feeling sick or, in more extreme cases, problems with sight or hearing. Discuss the importance of relaxing when performing and then get your pupil to consciously practise performing a piece in as relaxed a frame of mind as appropriate. During the actual performance concentration should be as focused as possible. Talk about the inner voice, which sometimes may be helpful ('keep the pulse steady'; 'listen carefully'; 'let's flatten that note just a tad'), or which may sometimes be less than co-operative ('there's that difficult bit coming up, I'm sure it won't go well'; 'played a note wrong, this performance really is not going well' and so on). If pupils do 'talk to themselves' in performance discuss ways of trying to encourage their comments to be positive and helpful rather than negative or off-putting!

If the music has been well prepared then nothing should go wrong. Teach your pupils to relax and to put trust into their preparation. Discuss these topics fully; there is a certain therapy in simply bringing these thoughts out into the open. You might assemble a group of pupils together – perhaps those taking an exam or performing in a concert – and use the questions above as a stimulus for a group discussion.

There are, of course, many ways in which to minimize anxiety. In the preparation for a performance or exam ensure that there is ample time to learn the material and that it is learnt *thoroughly*. All technical problems should be practised until they are entirely overcome. A performance will generate far less anxiety if the performer knows there are no technical weaknesses. Remind your pupils of that wise old saying 'the amateur practises until he gets it right; the professional practises until he doesn't get it wrong'. If the performance is to be accompanied, make sure that sufficient rehearsal time with a sympathetic accompanist is organized. Set up practice performances, both in front of small audiences and in the actual performance venue, if possible. If appropriate, ensure that the instrument is in optimum working order. Discuss and rehearse the 'theatre of performance' – walking on and leaving the platform, stage or performance area, acknowledging the audience both before and after the performance and, if appropriate, what to do during rests. Discuss dress. Leave as little as possible to chance.

Recommend that your pupil has a good night's sleep the night before a performance or exam. Cognitive ability and concentration are both dependent on an appropriate number of hours' sleep. On the day of the performance ensure that the way to the venue is known and that plenty of time is allotted for the journey. Anticipate other potentially stress-inducing problems: parking, money for a meter etc. In the ten or so minutes before the performance tell your pupils to take long, slow, deep breaths, breathing out slowly through the mouth. This will help to slow down the heartbeat and encourage a feeling of relaxation. Suggest that they sit very quietly and still for a few minutes, trying to focus their minds on being calm. The American psychiatrist, Charles Stroebel, devised an ingenious and simple method of dissipating anxiety. His technique, when anxiety begins to loom, is to:
- smile;
- take two very slow, very deep breaths;
- tell yourself, 'I'm calm!'.

It may well work for some!

## Playing from memory

There are many convincing arguments both for and against performing from memory. Whichever side of the fence you sit on, there is little doubt that the ability to play from memory is a useful one and should be taught to pupils, even if they don't actually do it in performance. Those who can find the confidence to present a performance without the notes in front of them may experience the music in a much more intimate way; they are truly 'at one' with the music. This will inevitably intensify and focus their ability to communicate it to their audience in a more vivid manner. Furthermore, it demonstrates clearly that the music has been studied in depth. In addition, having a number of pieces in the memory also means that pupils will be able to give impromptu performances, which will provide great pleasure for family and friends.

The workings of the memory, from a scientific point of view, are highly complex. From the point of view of the instrumental or singing teacher this is not important. Although the music teacher's concept of 'memory' is probably going to be a little over-simplified it is certainly sufficient for helping young players to develop this useful skill.

> Think of a piece you know from memory. Before reading on, consider how many different ways you 'know it'?

You will probably have thought of the following:
- the sound of the piece, which you can, as it were, 'play back' through your inner ear;
- the feel of the piece in your fingers;
- the look of the notation in your 'mind's eye';
- the feelings or emotions the piece causes you to experience.

In essence, these are the various ways that pupils can be taught to memorize music. Playing successfully from memory will result from using a combination of the following methods.

### Aural memory
Knowing how the music sounds in your head, and being able to 'sing' it through internally, are strong memory motivators. Suggest that when pupils hear the piece through their inner ear they try to include shaping, dynamic levels and tone quality. Particular phrases (especially tricky ones) can be thought through, imagining the fingering.

### Kinaesthetic memory
This kind of memory, also known as muscular memory, will develop as a piece is repeated over and over again. It is important that the music is learnt very accurately, however; since this type of memory depends on one physical action leading to another, any mistakes that have been practised will be very difficult to undo. One problem with this form of memorizing is that if something does go wrong in performance, it may be very difficult to re-establish the musical thought and continue the performance. It is therefore important to identify certain strategic points in the music and ask your pupils to practise beginning from each of those points.

### Intellectual memory
Each piece being learnt from memory needs to be understood. In a simple piece this may mean no more than knowing the overall structure and some basic harmonic and cadential points. For the more advanced player this may mean undertaking a detailed analysis of the work. Pupils should

look carefully at similar sections in the piece, and note the differences. These passages will require careful and conscious control. Pupils should also be able to talk their way through salient features of the music, rather like narrating a story.

**Photographic (visual) memory**
A few lucky individuals are blessed with what some call a 'photographic memory'. They can, as it were, 'see' a mental image of the printed music in their 'mind's eye'. There are, however, problems associated with this form of memorizing – the image can be disturbed during a complicated technical passage or, if the occasion arises, when following a conductor, or as the result of some other distraction. In addition, it is virtually impossible to teach. If a pupil does seem to possess this gift, make sure that any memory work is strongly backed up by one or more of the other memory methods discussed above.

There are further strategies for memory practice with which you may like to experiment:
- Passages that cause particular trouble can be played slowly, beginning on different notes (e.g. transposed up or down a tone or semitone). This will really focus the ear and help establish the precise shape. Certain technically tricky passages may often cause a pupil to falter because they simply look difficult. Learning to play such passages from memory immediately removes the visual element and suddenly the difficulty may be vastly reduced.
- Sing particular sections. Play one phrase, then sing the next, proceeding in this way throughout the piece. Then reverse the process.
- 'Play' the piece through in your imagination.
- As an extreme test, at least of kinaesthetic memory, try reading (aloud if your instrument permits) from a book or newspaper for the duration of the performance. Then try to repeat (from memory!) the substance of what has been read.
- Perhaps the most important advice you can give is that the quickest way to play accurately from memory is to practise slowly.

# Chapter 16

# Examinations

## The role of grade examinations

There is no denying the great importance attached to exams in today's society. However, we should not simply jump on the exam 'band-wagon' without having first carefully thought through and questioned their true function. Why do we put our pupils in for exams and what exactly are they being examined for? Are these tests indeed a fair assessment of a developing musician's ability?

In the teaching of musical instruments the great majority of teachers use the grade and diploma system of music exams to form the basis and structure of their teaching. It would seem to be very important, therefore, that we are convinced that they do indeed fulfil their function and succeed in what they set out to achieve – that they really *are* a fair assessment of the candidate's ability.

There are certain broadly accepted functions of instrumental music exams. Perhaps the most important is that they offer a powerful source of motivation: by passing an exam pupils have risen to a challenge and they can then go on to study more demanding and exciting repertoire, or perhaps join an orchestra or ensemble. In other words, the exam has set up a strong incentive to continue their studies. In addition, it is also generally accepted that exams:
- demonstrate and maintain a reasonably consistent and measurable standard of performance;
- chart the approximate musical and technical ability of a student against an existing set of perceived standards, which enables teachers and pupils to monitor progress;
- offer some useful feedback to the pupil (often reinforcing points made by the teacher time and time again!);
- form a point of consolidation and focus for a pupil's work and present both the opportunity and necessity to bring pieces and the supplementary studies and technical work to as high a standard as possible;

- present an opportunity to perform in front of an independent and unbiased professional musician;
- help to structure a course of study;
- ensure that general musical aspects are not neglected, but developed alongside the playing of pieces;
- help pupils to develop technique by the inclusion of studies, scales and arpeggios.

## Misusing examinations and failure

It is also important to be aware of the disadvantages that may result if the exam system is misused. Perhaps the most common problem occurs when pupils are fed a diet of exam material to the exclusion of anything else. The teacher who simply presents pupils with one exam after another will cause a kind of musical malnutrition, which in turn may well lead to a stunted musical growth.

Entering candidates without due consideration may give rise to all sorts of problems. Try to ensure that their general musical ability is appropriate to the grade in question. Never enter a pupil simply to 'make them work' (unless you both agree on this as a positive strategy!) and, at least to the best of your knowledge, avoid entering candidates whom you feel may fail. It is well to remember that exams are, first and foremost, for the benefit of the pupil – not the teacher or the parent! Putting a pupil through the exam process for the personal or professional benefit of the parent or teacher is highly inadvisable.

Awareness of the most recent syllabus is essential – never enter a candidate on the basis of an old syllabus; syllabuses change and it is your responsibility to be aware of such changes. The appropriate preparation time is important: for the weak candidate too little may be the cause of failure, whilst the good candidate may fail because boredom sets in, causing performances to become stale and lacking in sparkle.

Failure, for whatever reason, is disheartening, discouraging and demoralizing for both teacher and pupil and so the decision whether or not to enter a pupil must not be taken lightly. Grade exams are designed to test all-round musicianship – if a pupil just wants to play pieces, then it's perhaps better just to let them play pieces. Certainly, pupils should never be entered for grade exams against their will; there is no doubt that a lot of hard work is a prerequisite for doing well and if pupils are not at least reasonably keen to take the exam, they certainly won't be prepared to put in the necessary effort.

## Preparing pupils for grade examinations

There is no doubt that the grade-exam syllabus can form a very solid basic structure for a teaching course, especially if it is used with care and imagination. We have already mentioned the importance of not moving from one exam to another, and the best time to enter a pupil should come:

- after suitable recovery time from the last exam (if there was one), followed by
- a full discussion of the work required with your pupil, and then
- after alerting the parent, who will probably be footing the bill!

During the exam term look at pieces outside those being prepared for the exam. You might perhaps be teaching two pieces from each list, and only towards the actual exam date make your final decisions, or you might simply sight-read through other repertoire at each lesson. The benefits of extra technical work are obvious; use scales and other exam material as a basis for improving all-round technique. It's not just a matter of playing the scale correctly, but of encouraging pupils to develop their tone, general control and fluency in their scale preparation. The benefits of *regular* sight-reading are dealt with in Chapter 7.

◀ **Chapter 8**
Teaching Scales

◀ **Chapter 7**
Teaching Sight-Reading

Good teachers will always try to set up opportunities for performing exam and other pieces – the more often the better. Here are some ideas:

> Encourage parents and other relatives to take an interest and listen to pieces (and scales!).
>
> If you have several pupils taking an exam in a particular term, get them together and have a group lesson in which they play to each other and discuss their performances.
>
> Arrange a mock exam (or more than one for the more nervous candidate). The first might be, say, three or four weeks before the exam and may well identify how the final few lessons could be best spent and how practice should be structured.
>
> Another mock exam, say, one or two weeks before the real one should be more of a confidence-building exercise (perhaps best avoided if you feel your pupil may not do so well). You might like to be 'the examiner', or you may have a friend to take on the role, or even ask one of your more advanced pupils, for whom the experience will be a very good lesson in general musical awareness and aural skills.

## Non-musical factors

There are many matters exerting influence over both exam preparation and performance that are not related to actual musical ability.

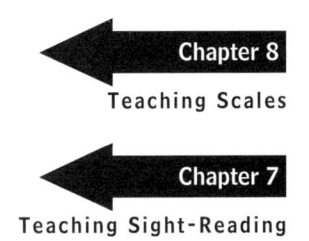

Candidates, as you would expect, react in their own individual way to these particular influences. So, even though you might teach the material efficiently, and indeed effectively (taking into account the differences in learning speed, musicianship and the other variables from one pupil to another), you might still find a broad range of response. It is therefore useful to have an idea of these non-musical factors. Some, you may be able to work to the advantage of the pupil, and awareness of others may help you to empathize with a particular pupil's problems. Some, you may simply not be able to do anything about. Here are a number of the main factors; the list is by no means exhaustive and you may wish to add further points:

- Candidates who have a positive attitude, and show persistence in their work, are always likely to do better than those who are more poorly motivated.
- Each individual deals with the pressures and strains of exams in different ways. Those with self-confidence will do better than those who suffer from nerves and a lack of self-assurance.
- Candidates may be experiencing specific social or emotional problems near the exam time. Adolescence, girlfriend/boyfriend troubles, problems at home or difficulties with other work may affect performance.
- Parental support (or lack of it) can be quite significant. You may be reminded of that famous, but probably apocryphal story – 'Mummy says if I pass my exam then I can give up!'.
- There may be a necessity to pass the exam as part of another exam (such as 'A' level or university/college entrance).
- There may be an element of luck at the exam itself – the scales the examiner asks for may just happen to be the candidate's favourites, or the examiner might stop the candidate just before a passage that had never really been fully controlled.
- A disturbance outside the exam room may cause a break in concentration; a reed or instrument might go wrong; the pupil might be going down with a cold; the music stand might fall down; the piano stool might break . . .

There is always an element of unpredictability in the outcome of an exam owing to one or more of these non-musical influences. However careful you are, you may be certain that *something* unexpected will happen somewhere along the way! To be forewarned is to be forearmed.

## The result

If pupils have been well prepared, and if the preparation has been rich in musical variety and experience, then whatever the result, the system has been put to effective use. Music, because of its very nature, can never be entirely objectively assessed; we are not dealing with measurable factors; style and interpretation are largely a matter of individual taste. Indeed, even those factors which may be considered entirely objective, such as exactness of pulse, rhythm and intonation, can still be the subject of disagreement. It is perhaps beneficial to discuss these points with candidates and to explain that although the result does not represent a precise indication of their abilities, it is a very useful guide.

## After the examination

For many pupils preparation for an exam will mean more intensive practice than usual, and this will require a fair amount of time and energy, both psychological and physical. Consequently, there will need to be a period of relaxation after the exam. 'Fun' repertoire can be studied, or it may be possible to spend more time playing duets or other ensemble music. Perhaps it might be a good time to explore some aspects of improvisation or composition. Before taking the decision to begin work on the next exam, use the period to develop facets of technique that may otherwise be neglected (or not usually approached in a really thorough manner), or explore styles of music not usually studied for exam purposes. In this way *you* remain in control rather than allowing the exam system to control you.

## Grade 8 and beyond

Many pupils now reach Grade 8 at quite an early age; this in itself raises an important question. It goes without saying that pupils should not be pushed through the grades at an unnatural pace; the reasons have already been stated, but it may well be even more tempting with particularly talented players. Grade 8 is an exam that requires the development of all-round musicianship and it expects a high degree of musical maturity that, in many cases, will only emerge with time. Even those with fluent and advanced techniques may have trouble doing really well if their ability to express themselves musically is not similarly advanced.

You may find that you do have a number of pupils who began at an early age, have worked consistently, with real enthusiasm and involvement, and have achieved Grade 8 around the age of 15 or 16. What then do you do with them in the sixth form? Many of the exam boards now offer a performing exam somewhere beyond Grade 8, but not demanding as much as a diploma. They go under different names: Performer's Certificate and Recital Certificate are examples. Each has its own requirements, so it would be wise to look at all the available choices before making your final decision; they may well be very appropriate for the musical and enthusiastic sixth former who wishes to take their studies further.

For those real enthusiasts, or those who wish to consider music as a career, it may be possible to sit a diploma whilst still at school. Such an exam demands a high level of both technical proficiency and musicality.

## Chapter 16

There may be paperwork involved, so it will be advantageous to be taking music at 'A' level or an equivalent exam. Shop around carefully – there are many different diplomas, each with different emphasis to suit different pupils. There are performing diplomas and, usually for those over 18, diplomas in teaching. If you do not do much teaching at this level and perhaps feel lacking in experience (but do have a pupil wishing to enter for a diploma) it would be reasonable and professional to arrange for your pupil to have an occasional lesson with a professor from one of the conservatories. This would in no way undermine your own skills, but demonstrate your integrity as a teacher and your care and concern for your pupil.

# Competitions and Festivals

When discussing their opinions of competitions and festivals, most musicians seem to fall firmly in one of two camps. For some they are seen as good sources of motivation; for others they represent a form of competitiveness unacceptable in the world of art.

## The advantages of competitions and festivals

Like exams, preparing for a performance in a competition or festival focuses work and leads to a public performance. Indeed, such occasions may provide some pupils with their only public performances during their school years. By virtue of participating, pupils will have the opportunity to hear other performers of varying ages, listen to unfamiliar repertoire and learn from, and perhaps meet, distinguished adjudicators. Performances may act as a trial run for a grade or school exam.

Some pupils may enter ensemble classes – a wonderful way to exercise their musical skills, working and performing with other like-minded musicians. Rehearsals, either with or without tuition, are likely to be musically stimulating, and there will be the added benefit of receiving useful feedback and advice from an experienced professional.

At the festival itself good adjudicators will probably reinforce points repeatedly made by teachers and should both enthuse and inspire. For the teacher it can be a rare occasion to sit back and listen objectively to the results of weeks, or even months, of preparation. Pupils can act unpredictably under such circumstances, and for those who may have decided on a musical career, it is important to assess this for the future.

Ultimately, entering pupils for competitions and festivals may simply act as confirmation of the efforts of the committed and enthusiastic teacher.

## The disadvantages and how to deal with them

In general, the major disadvantages all relate to the competitive element. It is all very well winning, but what about the losers? Of course, music-making is not a sport and it is very difficult to justify a 'first-past-the-post performance'. 'Winning' at music is a very artificial concept and becomes more so as the stakes rise. A sympathetic and intelligent adjudicator will know how to handle this situation. In competitive music festivals around the country there is now a move towards a less competitive ethos, with gradings such as 'outstanding', 'very good', 'promising' and 'insecure', rather than meaningless marks. There will be winners and losers, but never forget that the result is normally one person's opinion of one particular performance. If teachers prepare their pupils well 'psychologically' and they enter with that well-worn spirit of 'it's not the winning, it's the taking part', then any damage caused should be very limited indeed. Another very important thought to instil in pupils is that the winners are not necessarily the 'best'. There are so many facets of musical ability that there will inevitably be a time and place for everyone, at some point, to 'do their best' and possibly even 'be the best'. In fact, comparison with other performers has very limited meaning; it is much better to view a performance as a comparison with oneself, with one's own 'best'. In this way no one can ever be a loser.

In a junior competition the winner will probably be the performer who gets the most notes correct, plays the rhythms fairly accurately, puts dynamic variety into their performance and bows courteously at the end.

It is a relatively straightforward task for the adjudicator to spot that performance, and those taking part and their parents will, in general, be in agreement. At the senior end of the spectrum, where the winner has to be decided from perhaps a highly competent and experienced pianist, cellist or trombonist, the situation is very much more complex. Participants, parents and teachers must realize that subjective opinion must rule – however objective the adjudicators might seem to be. The complexity of response, compounded when there is a panel of adjudicators, may produce virtually any result; it is therefore imperative that participants enter such competitions in the right spirit.

## Preparing pupils

The choice of music to be played is important, perhaps the most important criterion being that it suits the temperament and ability of the pupil. For the willing but anxious pupil, choose music that is well within their grasp – that they can enjoy playing. For the more determined pupil you may choose something that represents a challenge. If the pupil is entering a 'recital class', then ensure that there is a good variety of tempo and style in the chosen pieces.

Make sure that the pupil is given the opportunity to perform in front of other pupils, or family and friends. Make sure that pupils have ample experience of playing with the accompaniment, if there is one. Discuss the whole 'theatre of performance': the pupil's deportment, both before and after the performance, and, if appropriate, how to acknowledge the accompanist.

Discuss the ethos of competitions: talk about the advantages of taking part, about winning and not winning, about the fact that there are no such things as losers in this context, about how the adjudicator's decision is a personal one.

Pupils will greatly appreciate your attendance at the event. You may be able to share in the glory of their doing well, or you may have to reassure them if nerves or some other factor resulted in disappointment. Choose interesting, perhaps unusual, repertoire. It will be a breath of fresh air for the adjudicator.

## High-profile competitions

Events that receive radio or television coverage put competitions into a new league again. Many of the organising committees of the existing competitions are very aware of the various psychological problems participants may have to deal with – from the potential confusion and turmoil of winning to the potential damage that disappointment can bring. Entrants can therefore expect to be treated with a certain degree of care and attention.

Unlike competitive festivals, which are primarily aimed at the amateur, these competitions are generally aimed at the aspiring professional. In the case of the former, it is most likely that the impetus for entering will come from the teacher (or possibly the parent). On the other hand, it should be the participant themselves who makes the decision to enter one of the advanced competitions, and here it really is very important to discuss at length what that person expects to get out of the exercise.

Many of these competitions now include masterclasses, workshops and other 'learning' experiences in order to lessen the competitive element and bring it more into focus with contemporary educational thinking. These are great plus points and should help benefit a greater number of people.

## The competitive world

There is no getting away from competition if one intends to remain part of normal society. It is salutary to think through any single day and note the number of competitive situations that you may face. The world of music and musicians is fraught with competition and for young players, who may well go on to become professional musicians, it seems to be no bad thing to get them accustomed to it. There is no shortage of stress-inducing competition among music students, be they at secondary or tertiary level, and this often carries through into professional music-making. Thus, the ability to recognize and deal with competition is yet another 'life-skill'; entering music festivals is as good a way as any to begin to come to terms with it.

# Holiday Courses

## Orchestral courses

For enthusiastic young players of orchestral instruments, attending holiday courses will probably be a source of considerable motivation, stimulation and pleasure. There are many local orchestras, often of a very high standard, and teachers will recommend appropriate pupils for audition. Once pupils have a reasonable grasp of technique, if they can sight-read proficiently and if music is important to them, you should discuss, with both pupil and parents, making an application. Many of these courses are residential so there are certain considerations to take into account:

- What is the cost?
- Is the pupil comfortable with staying away from home?
- Does the pupil get on easily with others?

Once the decision has been made to apply, you will need to discover the entry criteria. Some courses are run on a simple 'come along' basis, others will require entry by audition. In the case of the latter, pupils should be prepared to play one, or possibly two, contrasted pieces, and should expect to do some sight-reading. Careful preparation will pay dividends, and particular emphasis should be placed on quality of sound and intonation. Pupils should be prepared to answer questions about their musical interests and to talk about any pertinent prior experiences.

## Other courses

There is almost no area of musical activity or study that does not have some kind of course for those keen to further develop their interests. These include:
- chamber music
- composition
- specific instruments
- early music
- jazz
- contemporary music
- choral singing
- recording
- music technology
- courses about composers
- opera
- pop music courses

Details of such courses will be found in any good music directory.

## Do-it-yourself courses

Enthusiastic teachers may consider running their own courses. Here are two possible scenarios:

> **Scenario 1**
> A piano teacher with a practice of 20 to 30 pupils might, for example, book a small local hall or music room in a local school for a day. The morning session may begin with a group discussion on technique in which various pupils play exercises, scales, talk about the problems of practising and discuss interesting new repertoire. Following a short break, the pre-lunch session delves into the mysteries of improvisation and composing.
>
> After packed lunches are consumed the assembled pianists discuss the ins and outs of sight-reading, concluding with some mock sight-reading exams. Finally, after a short break for a drink and snack the day could end with a concert, in which everyone plays a short piece to the other participants and their parents.

A small charge to cover hiring the hall and paying for drinks and snacks would not deter supportive parents from such a day.

> **Scenario 2**
>
> A wind teacher has between 40 and 50 pupils and obtains permission to use the music department of a local school for a small fee for a weekend. The first morning begins with the whole group playing ensemble music together.
>
> After the morning break there is a group discussion on technique during which such aspects as posture, breathing, scales and how to practise exercises are covered. After lunch everyone is divided into smaller (carefully prearranged) groups and sent to various rooms to rehearse – clarinet and flute quartets, mixed trios etc. The teacher, who will probably need one or two helpers for this, goes round the groups giving help and advice. After a short tea break everyone assembles for a short concert of the various groups.
>
> The second day begins with a visit by a musical celebrity who gives a short series of 'masterclasses' for a variety of pupils (of all standards) or possibly an illustrated talk on performing, how to tackle technical problems (or whatever). After a break there is another mass play-in. In the afternoon there is a short group discussion on preparing for performances and exams.
>
> To conclude the weekend, there is a short concert for parents and friends, which includes a piece for the entire ensemble, one or two of the group pieces rehearsed yesterday and some solos.

An enormous amount of work for the organizer? Certainly! But what a wonderful weekend for all who take part. The cost? Hiring the department, a celebrity for a morning, some drinks and snacks and other miscellaneous costs. Split 45 ways, it should not be too expensive.

# What Next?

## Music college or university?

If a pupil is determined to study music at tertiary level, their first major decision will be between music college and university. Inevitably, the perceived difference is that music college is for those who wish predominantly to perform and university is for those with a more 'academic' interest in music. In essence this is indeed the case. However, the dividing line is becoming less distinct, with university courses offering significant practical components and music colleges, often in conjunction with nearby universities, offering significant academic components.

In helping to make the decision for the 'performing' musician, there are two particular considerations to take into account:
- What is the standard of orchestral and chamber music?
- How much time will be available for practice?

It may well be that the answers to these questions influence your pupil in one direction or the other. For the aspiring performer, music college may be the right choice. These institutions will have a greater number of professional musicians on the staff, there will be frequent visits by international artists, and the courses themselves will be geared to preparing for professional musical life. Many courses have taken the latter point quite seriously and offer advice on self-promotion, dealing with prospective employers and numerous other vocational areas.

A university course, on the other hand, will include subjects such as music history, musicology, analysis, ethnomusicology, aesthetics, composition and music technology. It may also offer opportunities to approach music in different ways, such as 'music as science' or 'music in society'. All universities prepare their own courses and the content and relative proportion of different subjects within a course is often quite diverse. Prospective students therefore need to send off for prospectuses and study them carefully.

## Chapter 19

For a 'performing' musician considering university, it is important to look closely at the actual weighting of practical music within the syllabus; it may constitute only a relatively small part. However, a number of universities now entertain such flexibility as to allow individual students a degree of opportunity to tailor the shape of their own particular course. It will also be necessary to decide with whom pupils will study, and whether there will be any travel involved. In addition, the student will need to establish who will pay for these lessons and whether there is the possibility of a subsidy.

Prospective music students can get advice from their schools and instrumental teachers. Most colleges and universities offer 'open days', and pupils would be well-advised to attend one or two to 'get a feel' for their proposed course of study and for the environment in which they may be spending the next three or four years. In addition to studying prospectuses, they should try to talk to present or former students of their favoured institutions.

When you decide on a music college, an important factor will be the specific teachers. A pupil may apply for a particular college because they very much wish to study with a particular teacher. There is nothing unprofessional about getting in touch with that teacher and arranging a 'consultation lesson'. Much may be learnt in this way, which may affect the final decision over the application. However, many colleges will not guarantee your first-choice teacher and it is definitely worth checking this carefully.

Some pupils, who attach virtually even weighting to both their practical and academic studies, and may be undecided exactly which direction to take, could be offered places at both music college and university. Under these circumstances they may like to take up the university course first and then go on to music college as a postgraduate, thereby getting the best of both worlds. It should, nevertheless, be taken into account that the standard required for entry to music college as a postgraduate is usually very high, *very* competitive and that these courses are very expensive. Music college followed by university is a less desirable strategy. A number of music colleges offer combined courses with local universities; these courses are normally very challenging and are not for the faint-hearted. In addition, they vary enormously in their provision for lessons and performing opportunities and should therefore be examined very carefully.

## Getting in

Entry requirements differ from one university music department to another, and should be well understood when applying. In the United Kingdom all will expect a good pass at 'A' level music and good grades, sometimes in one, but normally in two, additional 'A' levels. Not all universities will require personal attendance at interview, but it is most strongly advised that pupils do not accept a place at a university they have never visited. If pupils do have to attend an interview, they should expect to be asked detailed questions about their musical life and interests, and perhaps to be quizzed on their musical knowledge. They may also be expected to perform.

Entry to music college is always by rigorous audition, and pupils should be equal to the stresses and strains of such a process if they intend to apply. By the time the auditions take place pupils should have had considerable experience of such occasions, having participated in competitions and festivals and taken many exams. It is salutary to note that these auditions are barely a year after entry to sixth form. It goes without saying that the pieces chosen should be prepared to the highest possible standards; it is usually a good idea for pupils to prepare comfortable repertoire, nothing too difficult, and make sure they have a number of trial runs. Pupils should also carefully think through their aims and future aspirations for discussion at interview.

## Other careers in music

There are of course many different types of careers available within the music world in addition to performing or teaching. These include:
- music administration (which may be connected to musical venues, associations, orchestras, chamber ensembles and so on)
- music publishing
- music retailing
- instrument manufacture
- recording
- music therapy

If you have a pupil interested in such a career in music, the best way forward is to get in touch with a careers advisor or an appropriate organisation and set up an interview. Many tertiary colleges offer specialist courses that may be germane to the favoured career.

# Chapter 20

# Some Professional Considerations

## Working for yourself

The two key factors in functioning as an independent, self-employed or freelance instrumental or singing teacher are: avoiding isolation and the stagnation that may arise from it, and managing the financial issues that arise from not working during school holidays. The huge advantage that accrues to those who choose this mode of operation is the opportunity to manage your own time and thus perhaps to fulfil a professional performing engagement, or indeed career, which may not otherwise be possible. The younger teacher may be concerned principally about the need to maintain some personal freedom and earn enough money to survive, whereas the older teacher may be more concerned with the isolation factor.

Working independently may mean teaching in your own home or studio, travelling from one school to another, or visiting pupils in their own homes. The prudent individual will give some careful thought to the implications arising from these possibilities:

- Is an income that may be derived from term-time earnings only, and which is unlikely to include paid sick leave, sufficient?
- Does your household contents insurance cover teaching individuals and groups at home?
- Are you liable if a pupil suffers an injury whilst in your house (from, say, tripping over a rug)?
- Are you covered by insurance if you are unable to earn your living as a teacher (or player) because of physical incapacity or if you are suddenly unable to teach?
- What is the situation over providing for a pension?

In the United Kingdom the private teacher must also address the issue of income tax and National Insurance, and appropriate financial advice should be sought if the inevitably large and surprising tax assessment is to be avoided.

## Working in schools

Having considered the above, it may be that teaching instrumental lessons within a school is a more attractive proposition in terms of security, employment conditions and terms. It may also provide a structure in which to develop your pupils' (and your own) musical skills, in terms of ensemble playing. However, it doesn't give you the same flexibility as being your own boss.

As a visiting music teacher, it is important that you are aware of both the school's policy on admission of visitors and the very real difficulties that may occur when teaching in a one-to-one situation, in a small room, with an unglazed door. Many music teachers rely on touch to impart information quickly. It is, of course, much easier to press a child's finger on to the correct key, valve or string, rather than providing a verbal explanation, but in countries such as the United Kingdom, where the Children Act (1989) applies, the physical contact between teachers and pupils is not permitted. It would be as well to check out national laws regarding the relationship between teacher and pupil but, in general, it is safe to assume that the golden rule for teachers should be *no touching*.

If possible, avoid working with one individual when the door is closed, especially if there is no glazed viewing panel in the door. For non-keyboard players, if space permits, place a chair between you and the pupil. Certainly think carefully about your physical position in relation to your pupil(s) in what may often be a fairly confined space.

Clearly, the situation for the teacher working in his or her own home is, in some respects, different. It is also different if one or both parents are present during the lesson. Again, however, the advice remains the same and, laborious though it may seem, it is wise to ask the pupil's permission and to explain why you deem it necessary to touch a finger or arm.

## Contractual obligations

It is important to determine what your contractual obligations are, and to whom you are contracted. This will depend on the nature of your employment. The actual contract may be written or verbal. In either event, it is in your interests as an employee to clarify what may be required of you, both in the short and long term. All teachers are advised to join a professional organisation in order to protect their rights.

For the teacher working privately at home, it is equally important to establish, usually with parents, what you may reasonably expect of them and their child (your pupil) and what they may reasonably expect of you as the teacher of their child. You may wish to draw up a contract between you and the parent detailing length of lessons, mode of payment, and what happens in the event of either party cancelling a lesson.

# The school music curriculum

For too long, instrumental teaching has functioned in isolation from curriculum activity. A moment's reflection may lead us to see how strange it is that children have music lessons at school (class-based) but learn to play instruments outside the classroom environment (except perhaps for percussion and keyboards). As a result, they experience two distinct music curricula.

If these two paths could be brought closer together, it is highly probable that more effective learning would take place. Including composing and improvising in our instrumental teaching will reinforce both the classroom learning and the broader and deeper understanding of music which we know is needed if performance is to be meaningful rather than perfunctory. At the same time, if classroom activities make greater use of instrumental skills the quality of learning for both player and fellow learners will be enhanced.

Classroom work should include listening to and appraising the pupil's own work and that of others. This, of course, has a direct bearing on instrumental teaching in which the encouragement to self-evaluate should be paramount. Work in the classroom can be effectively complemented by group instrumental teaching, providing a seamless transition between class lesson, ensemble activity and instrumental teaching.

Try to gain a picture of what your pupil experiences in music lessons at school, by asking them questions such as:
- What activities take place in music lessons at school?
- How long are these lessons?
- How often are these lessons?
- Does singing feature in their school life?
- What kind of songs are sung and are pupils used to singing in parts?
- Are keyboards, recorders, guitars or percussion instruments used in the classroom?
- Are pupils ever asked to perform in the classroom?

You will already know about your pupil's extra-curricular musical activities and so, together with the above information, you can begin to build a picture of the importance of music in your pupil's life. Knowing that music is not terribly significant for your pupil, for example, will serve as a reminder of the importance of motivation, stimulation and the creation of as many extra-curricular musical opportunities as possible. As we move towards more open access to instrumental tuition, the onus of responsibility is very much on the teacher to provide the necessary opportunities, encouragement, stimulation, motivation and act as a role model, in order to allow each pupil a full and exciting musical life.

# Further Reading and References

*A Common Approach: A Framework for an Instrumental/ Vocal Curriculum* (England, Federation of Music Services (FMS)/National Association of Music Educators (NAME), 1998, distrib. Faber Music)

*Instrumental Teaching and Learning in Context: Sharing a Curriculum for Music Education* (England, Music Advisers' National Association (MANA); now NAME, 1995)

*The Arts in Schools* (London, Gulbenkian Foundation, 1982)

Aiello, Rita. *Musical Perceptions* (Oxford University Press, 1994)

Beale, Charles. *Jazz Piano from Scratch* (London, ABRSM, 1998)

Benson, Jarlath. *Working more Creatively with Groups* (London, Tavistock, 1987)

Butler, Gillian and Tony Hope. *Manage Your Mind: The Mental Fitness Guide* (Oxford University Press, 1995)

ed. Child, Dennis. *Readings in Psychology for the Teacher* (London, Holt, Rinehart & Winston, 1977)

Durrant, Colin and Graham Welch. *Making Sense of Music: Foundations for Music Education* (London, Cassell, 1995)

Entwistle, Noel. *Styles of Learning and Teaching: An Integrated Outline of Educational Psychology for Students, Teachers and Lecturers* (London, David Fulton, 1988)

Fontana, David. *Psychology for Teachers* (Basingstoke, Macmillan, 1995)

Gardner, Howard. *Frames of Mind: The Theory of Multiple Intelligences* (London, Fontana Press, 1993)

Green, Barry. *The Inner Game of Music* (London, Pan, 1987)

Green, Lucy. *Music on Deaf Ears: Musical Meaning, Ideology, Education* (Manchester University Press, 1988)

Hallam, Susan. *Instrumental Teaching: A Practical Guide to Better Teaching and Learning* (Oxford, Heinemann, 1998)

Hargreaves, David J. *The Developmental Psychology of Music* (Cambridge University Press, 1986)

Harris, Paul. *Improve Your Sight-Reading!* (London, Faber Music, 1994)

—*Improve Your Scales!* (London, Faber Music, 1999)

—*Perfect Your Sight-Reading!* (London, Faber Music, 2000)

Hefling, Stephen. *Rhythmic Alteration in Seventeenth- and Eighteenth-Century Music: Notes Inégales and Overdotting* (New York, Schirmer, 1993)

Jaques-Dalcroze, Emile. *Rhythm, Music and Education* (London, Dalcroze Society, 1967)

Kemp, Anthony. *The Musical Temperament: Psychology and Personality of Musicians* (Oxford University Press, 1996)

Kodály, Zoltán. *The Selected Writings of Zoltán Kodály* (London, Boosey & Hawkes, 1974)

Lovelock, William. *Common Sense in Music Teaching* (London, G. Bell, 1965)

Machover, Wilma and Marienne Uszler. *Sound Choices: Guiding Your Child's Musical Experiences* (Oxford University Press, 1996)

Meyer, Leonard B. *Emotion and Meaning in Music* (University of Chicago Press, 1961)

O'Connor, Joseph. *Not Pulling Strings* (London, Lambent Books, 1987)

Odam, George. *The Sounding Symbol: Music Education in Action* (Cheltenham, Stanley Thornes, 1995)

Oglethorpe, Sheila. *Instrumental Music for Dyslexics: A Teaching Handbook* (London, Whurr, 1996)

Pratt, George. *Aural Awareness: Principles and Practice* (Oxford University Press, 1998)

Reimer, Bennett. *A Philosophy of Music Education* (Englewood Cliffs, N. J., Prentice-Hall, 1989)

Schafer, R. Murray. *The Rhinoceros in the Classroom* (London, Universal Edition, 1975)

Seashore, Carl. *Psychology of Music* (New York, Dover, 1967)

Sloboda, John. *The Musical Mind: The Cognitive Psychology of Music* (Oxford, Clarendon Press, 1985)

ed. Spruce, Gary. *Teaching Music* (London, Routledge/Open University, 1996)

Sternberg, Robert and Janet Davidson. *Conceptions of Giftedness* (Cambridge University Press, 1986)

Storr, Anthony. *Music and the Mind* (London, Harper Collins, 1992)

Swanwick, Keith. *A Basis for Music Education* (London, Routledge, 1979)

—*Music Mind and Education* (London, Routledge, 1988)

—*Musical Knowledge: Intuition, Analysis and Music Education* (London, Routledge, 1994)

—*Teaching Music Musically* (London, Routledge, 1999)

Tomatis, Alfred. *The Conscious Ear: My Life of Transformation Through Listening* (Barrytown, N. Y., Station Hill Press Inc., 1992)

Westcombe, John. *Careers in Music* (Oxford, Heinemann/NAME, 1997)

# Attendance Register

Term beginning:

| Name | Form/Class | Age | Week 1 | Week 2 | Week 3 | Week 4 | Week 5 | Week 6 | Week 7 | Week 8 | Week 9 | Week 10 | Week 11 |
|------|------------|-----|--------|--------|--------|--------|--------|--------|--------|--------|--------|---------|---------|
|      |            |     |        |        |        |        |        |        |        |        |        |         |         |

# Pupil Profile Form

| | |
|---|---|
| Name: | Term beginning: |
| Age: | Date: |
| Instrument:      Make: | Serial number: |
| Address: | |
| Phone number: | |
| Last exam taken: | Mark: |

| | Assessment* |
|---|---|
| Posture | |
| Tone control | |
| Dynamic range | |
| Scales and arpeggios | |
| Intonation | |
| Practice | |
| Aural | |
| Improvisation | |
| Sight-reading | |
| Ability to memorize | |
| Motivation | |
| Punctuality | |
| General organization | |

*Excellent/Good/Satisfactory/Weak/Poor

Other musical activities (concerts/festivals/exams etc.)

Other interests

# Termly Overview Sheet

Pupil's name:

Term beginning:

**Musical and technical targets**

Pieces:

Studies:

Scales:

Technique:

Aural:

Sight-reading:

Other musical activities (concerts/festivals/exams etc.)

End-of-term assessment

# Lesson Plan/Record Sheet

**Pupil's name:**

Date:

Lesson notes/work to be covered:

Priorities for next lesson:

Work set:

| **Evaluation** | Practice: | Performance: | Progress: |

Date:

Lesson notes/work to be covered:

Priorities for next lesson:

Work set:

| **Evaluation** | Practice: | Performance: | Progress: |